3

CONTENTS

PAGE

SUPPLEMENT

EVANGELICAL RELIGION IN THE SCOTTISH HIGHLANDS

by Professor J Douglas MacMillan

FOREWORD

Old friends need no introduction and some may think that any introductory preface to this book, Murdoch Campbell's well known *Gleanings of Highland Harvest* is unnecessary. However, there are several matters that demand, and deserve, explanation in this new, and eagerly awaited, republication of a popular book which has too long been out of print and unobtainable on the second-hand market.

It was felt, for example, that some effort should be made to set the work more explicitly into its local and historical perspectives. It is written from within the focus of a very definite period and a very specific culture. It reflects upon, and interacts with, the spiritual life of the Scottish Highlands in the period following the Spiritual Awakenings of the mid-nineteenth century. This being so, it was felt that an outline of the historical background to the book would help present-day readers understand, and absorb, its atmosphere. At the kind invitation of the publishers I have been happy to attempt this task, and feel greatly privileged to be asked to contribute, even in a modest way, towards the re-issue of what I have always regarded as one of the best of my late, and greatly esteemed, father-in-law's devotional writings. Other reasons also dictated the provision of such a framework.

To begin with, the book was originally published as long ago as 1953, quickly reprinted on popular demand, and issued in a new and enlarged edition in 1958. While it makes an appeal over a wide front it was aimed, initially, at a constituency very familiar with, and historically not so terribly far removed from, many of the people, customs, and events with which it deals in its sensitive, and spiritually helpful way.

However, over the intervening years several things have happened which affect that situation. First, time has moved on and many of the people of whom the author writes, and the scenes which he so vividly depicts, now belong to a past with which even the Highland Christian is no longer so familiar. The last thirty years have seen many changes in Highland churches and the book takes for granted a familiarity with many customs and conditions now becoming a thing of the past. Mr Campbell had been in touch with people whose lives reached back to the events he describes. Today, only those Christians who have special historical interests are likely to be well informed about those people and their times.

A new generation of younger Christians, for instance, feels quite remote now from men such as Principal John MacLeod, Professor John R. MacKay and others whom Mr Campbell discusses and also uses as sources of information from the past. Those two particularly, from among his teachers in the Free Church College Edinburgh, were still vividly remembered by the first readers of *Gleanings*. Men who loomed large in the spiritual life of the Free Church of Scotland through the first decades of this century, they did much also to shape his own Christian outlook and mould him as an outstanding preacher and fine writer. Now they are only figures of history to most of us and sadly the story of their own faith and deeds is not readily available.

Second, Mr Campbell's name is known over a much wider front than it was even when he re-issued the last edition of this work in 1958. Other writings which followed this one reached the Christian book-market at a time when there was a new demand for Christian literature. His lucid style, biblical belief, and reformed doctrine and his deeply spiritual, experiential and devotional writing won him an international Christian readership, and some of his books have been translated into other languages. Without doubt, the wider readership will wish to take advantage of this reprint of *Gleanings*. For such readers, it has been felt necessary to shed some further light upon the culture, circumstances, and historical development of the

Christian life of the Scottish Highlands and Islands with which the book deals.

Thirdly, were Mr Campbell alive to oversee this further issue of *Gleanings*, I feel quite certain he would have written some such historical background to it as I have tried to provide. My single regret is that he did not, himself, live to accomplish what he had sometimes contemplated and spoken about. He would have done it in such a way that it would have sat very easily and naturally with the rest of the book and his discussion of major events of Highland Church history, in which he was deeply versed, would have been a wonderful addition. However, even if his personal, spiritual touch is missed in that part of this book for which he bears no responsibility, I hope that my empathy with his work and outlook and love for him as a minister of the gospel, helper of my faith, and father-in-law will be evident in what I have written.

Finally, for readers who may not be familiar with Mr. Campbell's name or story some simple biographical details will also, doubtless, be welcome in rounding off this Foreword.

Murdoch Campbell was born in the parish of Ness on the northern tip of the Island of Lewis, the largest of the group which make up the Hebridean Islands of Scotland's North-West seaboard. His father, Alaistair Campbell was a crofter-fisherman, himself eminent for godliness, who became over the latter half of his life a full-time missionary with the Free Church of Scotland in Lewis, Harris and Skye. Murdoch Campbell was always conscious that he had entered into a remarkable spiritual heritage, and this was one of the elements of his life which gave him an abiding interest in God's work of grace amongst previous generations of his Highland and Island forebears.

Mr Campbell attended the village school in Ness until he was twelve, at which age the family removed to Berneray, Harris where his father took up his new work as a missionary. At seventeen, when he was still under military age, he volunteered for naval service, was drafted instead to the army, and saw military service until the end of the war, all in the same year, 1918. With that experience behind him, he then became a shipwright in the great shipyards of the Clyde and it was during this period that he underwent a strong spiritual experience of conversion to Christ which was to change, not only his heart but, ultimately, the whole of his future career. It was to mark his ministry, his preaching, his writing and it was to be precious to him all his days.

Of that experience he writes, very beautifully, in this way. "It was as if Someone had opened the long shut door of my heart and just walked in. My whole inward being was, as it were, invaded by a power which was both sweet and life-giving. It was a new thing which had never touched my spirit before. My consciousness was flooded by something like a gentle warm wave of light, life and love. God, I felt, had in mercy broken through the awful barrier of my sin, and had saved me from its dominion, guilt and power. He had, for Christ's sake, forgiven all my sins and cast them into the depths of the sea. He had forgiven and forgotten, but how much he forgave I may never know. He... changed me into a 'new creation'. My soul, like a restless dove, had now found its place of rest in the clefts of the Rock of Ages." *(Memories of a Wayfaring Man*, pp.22,23).

At the age of twenty-two he began studies at Skerry's College, Glasgow, and went on to graduate in Arts from Edinburgh University before studying theology at the Free Church College. In 1930 he was ordained and inducted into his first congregation in the beautiful parish of Fort Augustus, in the county of Inverness. That same year he married a lovely Christian from Strathpeffer, Mary Fraser, whom he met during his days as a student preacher in that area. She had sparkling beauty, intelligence and warmth and, like him, the character of a Highland natural aristocrat. Each had gifts and qualities the other lacked, and they fitted together as equals.

They had four children, two boys and two girls, but had the sorrow of losing their first child, Donald in early infancy. Their eldest daughter Anne retired from training handicapped children and is married to a Christian farmer in Ross and Cromarty; Mary, their second daughter, is married to the writer of these lines; and their second son David lectures in philosophy in Glasgow.

In 1934 Mr Campbell left his greatly loved people in Fort Augustus to take up the challenge of a fairly new, but busy, city pastorate in Partick Highland congregation, Glasgow. There he ministered to a large number of his fellow islesmen as well as people from other Highland areas and the city of Glasgow itself. During the Second War he served as Naval Chaplain at Portsmouth and Plymouth where his preaching was blessed to the conversion of many servicemen. His last ministerial charge was in Resolis, in the Black Isle, Ross and Cromarty, and there he was able to pursue a writing as well as a powerful preaching ministry. He was moderator of his Church's General Assembly in 1956.

A man of warm feeling and keen intellect, of real humanity as well as exceptional spirituality, Mr Campbell walked closely with God all his days. Like Jacob at Peniel, and like so many of those about whom he writes in this book, he enjoyed deep experiences of fellowship with his Lord as well as daily guidance through His Word. This element in his writing should neither surprise, nor be lightly dismissed by, any of his readers. Neither should we misconstrue it as narrow "Mysticism", nor yet as belonging to the sphere of "extraordinary charismatic gifts" - two extremes of outlook for which he would have had no sympathy at all. Again, this element is not confined to him but is, on the contrary, central to Christianity in some of its finest flowerings, as for example in the Highlands since the Reformation. That this is so is confirmed by the historical notes included in this volume.

As one who knew him intimately, in his private as well as his public life, I was always deeply impressed by one thing. This was the fact that his life, and faith were rooted in, and ruled by, the Scriptures as the infallible Word of God and, as was true of the Evangelical fathers in the Highlands of last century, it was only through the Word that he expected to hear his Master speak; but that, he did expect; and that, I am totally convinced, he did experience.

Mr Campbell was unusually gifted as a pastor and, in all his congregations, greatly loved by his people. He was, like Dr MacDonald of Ferintosh and Dr Kennedy of Dingwall last century, and of whom he speaks here, always in great demand as a preacher at Highland Communion seasons, and he himself loved being in the fellowship of the Lord's people on such occasions. As an evangelist he was superbly equipped and very often his word was "with power" to the quickening into spiritual life of individual hearers.

In another way, also his Master gave him a special gift and widely used him in its exercise, and that was in the work of personal evangelism flourishing in chance individual encounters. The plain fact is that he loved to talk about his Saviour and was an expert at drawing people, especially young people, into conversation about spiritual things. Nothing pleased him more than to see God's grace at work in the salvation of sinners. I am continually meeting people who tell me that he was the instrument, in God's hand, of their conversion to Christ.

He retired from the pastoral ministry in 1968 because of ill-health, and for his remaining years resided in Inverness. There, while health allowed, he continued to preach in the surrounding towns and villages as opportunity afforded and to the end, I believe, his preaching had God's blessing resting richly upon it. Finally, after months of increasing weakness, the Master he had loved and served so well took him home on 9th January, 1974, at the age of seventy-three years.

My last memory of him is of a final visit in the Infirmary in Inverness just a day or two before his homecall. He was extremely weak then, but mentally and spiritually alert. Of our conversation I remember and cherish every word and can say because of it, and of the Lord whose presence he still knew, that "his latter end was peace".

J Douglas MacMillan

What the Stranger Saw.

It might be of interest to mention how Highland religious custom impressed the stranger from the south who, over a hundred years ago, came across solemn scenes such as have been described by William Laidlaw and William Howitt. The two Williams apparently never met, but they each gave an independent account of what they saw. They were both gentlemen of learning and culture. Their reverent sympathy for that form of pure religion which brought such blessings to our forebears is far removed from some of our modern writers on Highland religious life. This is how William Laidlaw, Sir Walter Scott's friend, writes of a communion service at the famous ' Burn ' near Ferintosh, in Ross-shire.

' The people here gather in thousands to the Sacraments, as they did in Ettrick in Boston's time. We set out on Sabbath to the communion at Ferintosh, near Dingwall, to which the people resort from fifty miles distant. Dr. MacDonald, the minister, who attracts this concourse of persons, was the son of a weaver in Caithness (but from the Celtic population of the mountains there). He preached the sermon in the church in English, with a command of language, and a justness of tone, action, and reasoning—keeping close to the pure metaphysics of Calvin—that I have seldom, if ever heard surpassed. He had great energy on all points, but it never touched on extravagance.

' The Gaelic congregation sat in a dell or cleuch of a long, hollow, oval shape bordered with hazel, birch and wild roses. It seemed to be formed for the purpose. We walked round the outside of the congregated thousands, and looked down on the glen from the upper end, and the scene was really indescribable.

' Two-thirds of those present were women, dressed mostly in large, high, wide, muslin caps, the back part standing up like the head of a paper kite, and ornamented with ribbons. They had wrapped round them bright coloured plaid shawls, the predominant hue being scarlet.

' It was a warm breezy day, one of the most glorious in June. The place will be about half a mile from the firth, on the south side, and at an elevation of five hundred feet. Dingwall was just obvious at the foot of Ben Wyvis, still spotted with wreaths of snow. Over the town, with its modern castle, its church, and Lombardy poplars, we saw up the richly cultivated valley of Strathpeffer.

' The tufted rocks and woods of Brahan were a few miles to the south, and fields of wheat and potatoes separated with hedgerows of trees, intervened. Farther off, the high peaked mountains that divide the county of Inverness from Ross-shire towered in the distance.

' I never saw such a scene. We sat down on the brae among the people, the long white communion tables being conspicuous at the bottom. The congregation began singing the psalm to one of the old plaintive wild tunes that I am told are only sung in the Gaelic service. The people all sing, but in such an extended multitude they could not sing together. They chanted as it were in masses or large groups. I can compare the singing to nothing earthly, except it be imagining what would be the effect of a gigantic and tremendous Æolian harp, with hundreds of strings! There was no resisting the impression.

' After coming a little to myself I went and paced the length and breadth of the amphitheatre, taking averages and carefully noting, as well as I could, how the people were sitting together, and I could not in this way make less than nine thousand five hundred, besides those in the church, amounting, perhaps, to one thousand five hundred.

'Most of the gentlemen of the neighbourhood, with their families, were there. I enjoyed the scene as something perfect in its way, and of rare beauty and excellence.'

And this is William Howitt's testimony written in 1838.

'We thought ourselves fortunate in August, 1838, when we happened to fall in with the celebration of this annual ordinance in the Highlands. We were at Beauly, about a dozen miles west of Inverness, on Sunday morning, and were enquiring of the landlady of our excellent inn how far it was to the celebrated Falls of Kilmorack.

' "Oh," said she, " it is a bare two miles, and you will be just in time to see the Sacrament administered there in the open air to the Gaelic congregation."

'Most of the people were on foot, none was barefooted. On week days, we saw scarcely a woman with shoes or stockings, but to-day, none was without. And, with the exception that hardly one had a bonnet on, the young women were not much to be distinguished from those of our smartest towns. They all had their hair neatly braided and adorned with a comb of tortoiseshell. Many of them had silk gowns and handsome worked muslin collars, others were dressed in white . . .

'Just where the river issues from the cliffs overlooking the salmon leap, there juts out a lofty piece of tableland. That is the burial ground of Kilmorack, and there, as we approached, we beheld upwards of a thousand people collected and conspicuous in the bright and varied hues of Highland costume.

'We stood, and, for a moment, almost imagined we were come upon a band of the ancient Covenanters. A more striking picture we never saw.

'We entered the burial ground through a dense crowd and seated ourselves on the low wall built on the edge of the precipice over the river. Beneath a spreading tree near the garden wall stood a movable booth of wood. From this booth the minister was now addressing the assembly while two other ministers occupied a seat behind him.

'On his left stood his little kirk, and, on the green knolls above, his manse, and a few Highland huts . . .

'A more serious and decorous congregation never was seen.

'When those who had gone forward communicated, the minister again addressed them, and they retired from the table, and a fresh company took their place. Another minister then came forward and there followed a new succession of psalms, prayers and addresses.

'We left about three o'clock, but were told that not till six o'clock would the service close.

'Shortly after we left, the distant voice of the minister and the wild cadence of the Gaelic psalms, like the breezy music of an Æolian harp, reminded us that it was a sacred anniversary of a grave and religious people.'

Surely such scenes as those just related must have an unusual background. What was it that moved such multitudes to walk in all weathers over moor, mountain and stream—many of them walking a distance of thirty miles each way—to be present at the celebration of a religious ordinance?   There is but one answer.   God's Spirit had been moving among them.   They had therefore come to see the infinite value of their personal salvation, and of the unsearchable spiritual riches which the Gospel of Christ freely offered to sinful men.   They knew, as God had revealed, that the only alternative to the enjoyment of that blessing was everlasting sorrow.   Therefore they gathered on 'the mountain' where the Gospel of salvation was proclaimed by men who gave manifold proofs that they were 'chosen vessels' sent with 'good news from a far country.'

The delight with which the people drank from the well of life may be illustrated by the involuntary exclamations of a man from Skye who, as the Word was being preached, felt the joy of the Lord filling his heart.   'Oh,' he cried, 'that my wife and neighbours were here: Oh that everyone in the island were here—yea, and the whole world too!'

The words remind us of those of Christiana as she stood in sight of the Cross and saw Incarnate Love dying in her stead.

The Rev. Duncan Macgregor, who laboured for some years in Stornoway and who afterwards ministered at Ferintosh and Dundee, once described a communion season on the outskirts of Stornoway in Lewis: 'The congregation may be seen carrying forms, stools and chairs to the hallowed spot.   There they sit, wet or dry, during the five days of the solemnity, with a love and reverence for God's ordinances rarely equalled. . . . On a sacramental Monday we met a frail old man carrying a stool in his hand.   "What have you got there, Alister?"   "Oh," he said with tears, "my heart is sore taking the stool away!"

'There had Alister during these days been refreshed with draughts from the well of Bethlehem.   He felt it good to be there.   It was the gate of Heaven.   He therefore wept taking the stool away.'

Let me give one other instance of the drawing and converting power of the Gospel.   In an Argyllshire village a number of men used to meet on certain nights to drink ardent spirits. But the Lord was working in the land, and many were turning from the error of their way.   One night a member of the party failed to appear.   He had been convicted of his sin and was now rejoicing in God's salvation.   The band became smaller and smaller until at last only one man turned up at the old haunt.   'What has happened to them?   What did they find better than what they had?   I must go and see for myself.' Thus mused the last of the group.   He went, and before long he also rejoiced in God's gift of eternal life.

Such stories could be multiplied to show that behind the great gatherings which William Laidlaw and William Howitt had witnessed was the saving and drawing power of God through the preaching of Christ and Him crucified.

Early Sowings in the Islands.

SINCE so much has already been written about the spread of the Gospel on the Highland mainland it would be interesting to note at the outset who were the first bearers of the precious seed of the Divine Word to the isles. Lewis, our largest Scottish isle, was, till the arrival of men like Alexander MacLeod, Uig, Finlay Cook and Finlay Munro, shrouded in thick spiritual darkness. The ' vail ' over the eyes of the people was heavy indeed, and the coarse mixture of native superstition which they mingled with their primitive heathenism, made it heavier still. That vail, however, was destroyed by the power of the Gospel, and the light of a new and wonderful morning swallowed up the long night of spiritual death. The Lewisman who dreamt he saw a man arriving on his native shore with the sun resting on his shoulder was afterwards overjoyed when he actually saw the same man disembarking at Stornoway. He was that herald of the dawn, Mr. Alexander MacLeod, afterwards of Uig. It was, however, the circulation of the Gaelic Bible, and the avidity with which the people drank from the living oracles of God, that prepared the way for these men. Before their arrival there were signs of a spiritual spring day.

The great revival, which reached high water mark in Uig on that famous Sabbath in June, 1827, when John MacDonald, Ferintosh, preached to an immense congregation, marked the spiritual birth of a generation of Christians noted for their holiness of life, Christian steadfastness, and thirst for the Word. On that Sabbath such a powerful conviction was produced by the Word of God that during the singing of the last psalm only the preacher and the two precentors could take part. The preaching which dwelt on the sovereignty of God in the salvation of men, and which proclaimed the perilous state of every soul of man under wrath, produced that awe which rests on the human spirit when it stands in conscious guilt in the Presence of the Eternal. That this was no 'morning cloud' awakening may be proved by the wonderful fact that in the parish where this happened the stream of outward moral conduct remained untainted for a generation.

To illustrate the respect which men had for the ordinances of the Gospel in those times people from the parish of Uig were known to attend communion ordinances in Stornoway without making any purchase in town lest any should say they had gone there with that motive. They would walk home the long distance of over thirty miles on Monday, and return to town later in the week to buy the necessities of life.

In the Parish of Ness, at the other end of the island, Mr. Finlay Cook, who arrived there in 1829, laboured for four years. Apart from the services of the Lord's Day he regularly catechised the people and preached twice during the week to large congregations. The awakening which followed touched every part of the island except one parish. This revival also was remarkable for its lasting spiritual results, and the absence of undesirable emotional excesses. It was marked, however, by two characteristics—the one physical and the other spiritual. Some of those who came under 'the power of the world to come' would sometimes fall forward in a quiet faint, as if struck down by an invisible hand. Others had the power of making accurate prediction, as, for example, when a woman from Bayhead crossing the sea to Uig could tell her fellow travellers the Scripture from which Mr. Malcolm MacRitchie was to preach the following day. Unlike other times and places, however, these abnormal manifestations were taken to prove nothing unless the life otherwise adorned the doctrine of the Lord.

Mr. Finlay Cook, once speaking of the first fruits of the Gospel in Lewis, and in the north generally, said to his young friend, Angus Morrison, that a period of decline would follow in four successive 'reapings.' The first crop of Christians, he said, would be outstanding and conspicuous in their difference from a graceless world; in the next generation the difference would be less obvious. The next again could only be distinguished from the unsaved with difficulty, while the next after that could not be distinguished from the world at all. Many years afterwards, when Angus Morrison was an old man, he confessed to his young and brilliant friend, Mr. John MacLeod —afterwards Principal of the Free Church College—that he had lived to see such a spiritual decline in the north.

Like many others, Angus Morrison never listened to a preacher whom he could place before Mr. Finlay Cook. His rich, doctrinal sermons, with their powerful applications, he considered unsurpassed. They carried with them the theological flavour of the two men who most impressed him in his earlier years—Mr. Neil MacBride, Kilmorie, Arran, and the famous Dr. Love of Greenock and Glasgow. Brought up in his spiritual youth at the feet of such a man, and endowed with a metaphysical cast of mind to which methodical theological teaching made a strong appeal, it was no wonder that, at the end of his days, Angus Morrison should prefer the more doctrinal preaching of Mr. Hector Cameron, Back, to the powerful but experimental sermons of the godly Mr. Duncan MacBeath.

To appreciate how Mr. Cook stood in the estimation of the Christian public of his time a Christian woman of discernment once remarked that Mr. R. Finlayson, Lochs, was the most 'affecting' preacher she had ever heard; Mr. John MacRae the most searching; Dr. John Kennedy the nearest to God in prayer; but Mr. Cook, in his presentation of the Word, the most evangelical. Though solid in his doctrine, Mr. Cook was by no means a colourless expositor. His sermons were frequently lit up by vivid and memorable illustration. In this respect he differed from his renowned brother, Archibald, whose sermons, though incomparable in their intense spirituality and searching power, are quite lacking in illustrative material.

Let us see how Mr. Finlay could illustrate his theme. Speaking on one occasion about the sprinkling of the blood on the night in which the Lord was to pass over Egypt to slay the first-born, he described how some among the children of Israel might have reacted to the commandment of the Lord. One man, confident in his false security, concluded that since his home was so well built the destroying angel could not harm it. He need not sprinkle the blood. Another thought he could deceive the angel by sprinkling something which resembled the blood above his door. The third, a poor man, whose house was a miserable abode, and not worthy to be called a house, was afraid the angel would not spare it though he should sprinkle the blood as required. Expressing his fears to Moses this poor man was told to do as the Lord had said. When morning came, the cry of death could be heard in the homes of those guilty of presumption, while the poor man and his house were spared. Dealing with an untutored people, Mr. Cook could make an effective application of his message within the scope of such a fertile illustration as this.

In exhorting the people to obtain a personal assurance of salvation on the ground of God's faithfulness in the covenant promise, he said on another occasion, ' Though I should see inscribed over the face of the heavens, and over the face of the earth, the words—" Finlay Cook shall be saved "—I could not rely on such a testimony. When, however, I get this assurance from the Word of God, I may well be assured of my everlasting acceptance and safety. And why? Because heaven and earth shall pass away, but His Word shall never pass away.'

By way of comparison let me give a characteristic fragment from Archibald Cook's sermons. ' O my friends, it is a great thing to be brought to love a secret place . . . The soul may thus set himself apart for God from a spirit of thankfulness. O child of God, if the Spirit of grace gives you a glimpse of the sins which you had once, if you " look unto the rock whence ye are hewn, and to the hole of the pit whence ye are digged," and look at yourself as you were, lying in your blood in the open field, think of your deliverance, and what it cost God before you could be delivered out of that pit. The Son of God had to become a man of sorrows, and to be sacrificed in your room. He then passed by and said to your soul, " Live," and the soul was quickened; and perhaps you remember the first day you had a spiritual being. Will not that soul be filled with thankfulness, and be disposed to give himself to the Lord's service? Why, see the Psalmist, after he got deliverance from the pains of hell, he says, " What shall I render unto the Lord for all his benefits toward me? . . . I am Thy servant, and the son of Thy handmaid: Thou hast loosed my bonds." These bonds were chains that all the angels in heaven could not loose. Ah, sinner, there were two chains on the soul that would make the very devils miserable to all eternity, the chains of guilt and of the curse . . . Now, the saved soul, in setting himself apart for the Lord, as the fruit of the Saviour's choice of him, comes to see the end of his creation. What is the greatest honour that ever was put on a sinner of this world? Is it to be a king or queen? No, no. The greatest honour is to answer the end of his creation —to glorify God. The riches of the world, the honours of the world, are but a shadow in comparison with this. In whatever company he is, whether among the people of God, or among the world, if he sees the crown on the head of the Redeemer, and the world under foot, he counts it an infinite sweetness, an infinite comfort . . .'

In this manner did the excellent and prophetic ' Mr. Archie ' preach all his days. A woman from the district of Fort Augustus used to tell that she heard him once repeating the words

' eternity ' seven or eight times, and that the awe which seemed to rest on the people was indescribable.

When Mr. Finlay Cook left for Inverness in 1833 he was succeeded in Ness by that ' mighty man of valour,' the Rev. John MacRae, who laboured, off and on, in three Lewis congregations.   Mr. John MacRae was a son of thunder.   His dramatic and awe-inspiring sermons on the majesty of God, the unrelenting demands of His Law, the curse resting on every soul of man out of Christ, often transformed his Lewis congregations into ' a place of weeping.'   Yet when he came to apply the healing balm of Gospel grace none could be more tender. From the very beginning of his ministry John MacRae was supreme in oratorical power and spiritual fervour.   When he was Gaelic teacher at Uig, Mr. Alexander MacLeod asked him to address the congregation on a communion Sabbath after the tables had been served.   As he stood up to deliver his message, Mr. Robert Finlayson, Lochs, remarked to his friend the minister, ' Wait now till you hear how he will make chaff of all we have been saying here today.'

His forceful and vivid illustrations were usually drawn from such sources as his island audience would appreciate.   Once he preached a powerful sermon on the disloyalty of the Church to her Lord.   He spoke of the Son as bringing a complaint to the Father with respect to her lack of love to Him, and her proneness to wander out of the way.   The answer was, ' Wait Thou My Son, till we cast her into the stormy sea of tribulation, and before she reaches the black rocks at the bottom of the deep (" clachan dubha a' ghrunna ") she will turn to Thee again.'

When he came to grips with the awesome fact of sin as it touched the very honour and the very heart of God his genius could flash like lightning.   One day, as he expounded the words, ' They shall look upon Him Whom they have pierced,' he said: ' Every sin has its own sting, and every sting in every sin for which Christ suffered entered His very soul.   There is one sin, however, of such dread persistency, and of which it might be said that it has two stings. It is like the sharp piercing blades of a shears which are joined in the one handle. This is the sin of unbelief. With that sin many seek to strike the Son of God in glory under the fifth rib.'

Mr. MacRae's pastoral kindness was proverbial, and where he saw signs of real poverty he invariably sent relief. He once visited Angus Graham, a poor but godly man who lived on the east side of the island, whom he found refreshing himself with bread and water. To Mr. MacRae's remark about the plainness of the fare, the aged disciple said he had what the Lord had promised, and His blessing besides. When he returned to the manse that evening, where he saw the table laden with ample and varied fare, he would not touch the food till a goodly portion of it was sent to his poor but contented brother in the Lord.

His tenderness in ministering comfort to ' the afflicted soul ' often revealed itself as he addressed the Lord's Table. ' Your trials are like a strong wind blowing on a goodly tree. Not only will the force of adversity give exercise to all your graces, the result of which will be more fruitfulness, but it will also cause you to bow your head in Christian resignation. In such storms the dead tree will break, but not such as have in them the sap of grace.'

In speaking of the blessedness of those who mourn after a godly sort he once pictured an angel asking the Lord in Heaven: ' What sighing do we hear coming from the earth? ' ' That,' was the reply, ' is the sighing of my suffering people, and there is more music in it than in all the songs of angels.'

John MacRae himself was no stranger to trial. He once had a visit from a man who felt that his afflictions were almost unbearable in their severity. He poured his complaint into the sympathetic ear of his minister. When he had finished his sad tale, Mr. MacRae said: ' Friend, you know not what trials are.

If I were to tell you of mine you should then see that yours are light indeed.' By that strange way of knowing that others lie in deeper shadows than ourselves the man went his way greatly helped and reassured.

When Mr. MacRae was minister of Knockbain, Ross-shire, Hector Jack, of Strathconon, left early one morning to hear him preach. As he listened to the sermon Hector was amazed to find his own spiritual exercises so vividly and minutely described, but he still thought that Mr. MacRae might possibly be referring to somebody else. At this stage of his discourse, Mr. MacRae declared, ' Young man, you are still wondering if I am referring to somebody else, but no, I am referring to you who were so anxious last night lest you might sleep in, that you divested yourself of only part of your clothes.' Naturally enough, at this stage Hector Jack regarded the sermon as extraordinarily prophetic, but still persisted in thinking the description might be applicable to someone else in the congregation. It was then that Mr. MacRae raised his voice almost to a shout, by way of emphasis, saying: ' You are still thinking, young man, that I may be referring to someone else in this congregation. To put it beyond the shadow of a doubt for you, then, I am referring to you, who, in addition to what I have already said, prayed beneath the willow bush in your back garden before you left for Knockbain this morning.'

This climax made it plain to Hector Jack that ' the secret of the Lord is with them that fear Him,' and so he was overwhelmingly melted with a sense of gratitude to the Lord who had revealed his state to His servant.

During one of his journeys in Lewis he was passing one day, in the company, I think, of the Rev. Peter MacLean, through the lovely vale of Galson. Mr. MacLean drew his attention to the quiet pastoral beauty of the place. ' What a suitable place for prayer this is,' said Mr. MacLean. The characteristic reply was: ' No. A battleship would be a better place by far.'

Although Peter MacLean himself had an eye for the beautiful he preached with as much force and power as his friend. Let us in passing give one story of this worthy man. On his way home one evening from Cape Breton he joined a group on board ship who stood admiring the beauty of the setting sun. While expressing his appreciation of the grandeur of the scene, he went on to speak of Christ the Sun of Righteousness, who went down to the grave red in His sufferings in a sea of wrath, but who rose again in the fresh glory of an endless life. And that evening some heard him to their everlasting profit.

The stern note continued in Mr. MacRae's preaching to the end. When minister at Knockbain he once preached a powerful sermon in the presence of Dr. Aird, and Mr. John MacAllister, Kilbride, Arran. Dr. Aird spoke to his friend of the great ability and power displayed in the sermon. His colleague agreed, but with a remark expressing regret that he had not for a season sat at the feet of that calm and bright pulpit star—Dr. John Love. In the Church of God, however, the son of thunder is often as useful as the son of consolation.

Mr. Robert Finlayson, mentioned above, was also well known throughout the Highlands on account of the sanctity of his life, the fertility of his imagination, and his constant expectation of his Lord's return in glory. He was a man who could weave golden parables and create images which enabled his hearers to grasp the meaning of truths which are sometimes difficult to explain. To give an example of this, he once spoke on the 'eternal weight of glory' which the Church of Christ shall exchange in Heaven for her 'light affliction' in this life. He described how the creatures which inhabit the great deep are so free and vital notwithstanding the vast and perpetual weight of shimmering seas above them. In the deep they are in their element; and the deeper down they go the more free, the more joyous and vital they are. So in Heaven 'the new creature in

Christ' shall reach his eternal element; and under the eternal weight of glory, in an ocean of infinite peace and love, his life, freedom and joy, shall reach the pinnacle of their perfection and fulness.

Perhaps, however, the man who did more than any other in breaking up the fallow ground in the Islands was the famous layman, Finlay Munro, a native of Tain. After his conversion the Word of God burned like fire in his bones, and with his tongue set on fire from Heaven he travelled widely through the north. Wherever he went the power of the Lord was present to heal the people. Many were the signs which followed this good man's work.

Angus Morrison was among the great gathering who heard him preach on the top of the solitary hill, ' Muirneag,' in Lewis. His theme on that occasion was: ' And on this mountain shall the Lord make unto all people a feast of fat things, a feast of wines on the lees . . . well refined.' The effect of that sermon on Angus may be gathered from his own remark in after life, ' I wept enough that day to fill a vessel.' A young Christian woman from North Tolsta used to tell of how this herald of salvation dwelt especially on the ' refining ' which took place when ' the love which is better than wine ' flowed out through Christ's wounds when He died on the Tree.

Crossing once the moor between Ness and North Tolsta, Finlay drank milk at ' a lone shieling ' where a young married woman from Ness, Margaret Gunn, spent part of the summer on the pasture land with the cattle. Margaret was then a stranger to God. Before he left her he asked if he might see her marriage ring. As he held it in his hand he remarked solemnly, ' How like eternity is this ring: it has neither a beginning nor an end.' This simple word marked the beginning of Margaret's concern as to her state in the light of an endless eternity.

Margaret was a friend of Marion MacRitchie, to whom Principal MacLeod refers in his excellent appreciation of Finlay Munro.

He stayed one night with an affectionate friend, Donald Morrison, Fivepenny. In answer to his host's question in the morning as to how he rested, Finlay said that in the first part of the night the words, ' O my leanness, my leanness ' fastened themselves very painfully on his mind. Before the morning arrived, however, comfort came. It occurred to him that if God's mighty prophet had to complain of leanness of soul ' it was no wonder though poor Finlay Munro should mourn for a like cause.' He realised, in other words, that though ' poor in spirit ' he was in hopeful company.

The deep attachment to his person on the part of many who received a lasting blessing through the labours of this excellent man could be illustrated by one example. It was a young girl from Lewis, locally known as ' Pegi 'Nic Dhomhuill,' who once carried his few belongings to the Sound of Harris. This Hebridean Phebe saw over a hundred summers before she died at Sandwick, near Stornoway. Her love for Christ's wandering servant never abated to old age.

On one of his journeys Finlay preached to a large gathering at Barvas. Margaret MacLennan, a young woman from Shader, used to relate how on that occasion exception was taken to the soundness of Finlay's doctrine by a man present. It was a sore interruption coming from a person whom he much esteemed. The day was dull and overcast. When the man had finished Finlay turned to the people and said that as a sign that he had spoken the truth of God the sun in the sky would presently show itself for a brief moment, but that it would remain hidden for the rest of the day. Almost at once a rent appeared in the sky, and the sun, in two successive flashes, appeared to all only to retire for the rest of the day behind a heavy blanket of cloud.

A woman present at that meeting was so grieved at what seemed to be a permanent rift in the friendship between two brethren in the Lord that she took her own way to have them reconciled. The next time Finlay was in the district he lodged in her home. Without his knowledge she locked him in while she went for the other man. Alarmed at her agitated manner this man concluded that something had gone wrong in her household. When he was well within her bolted door she addressed them both, 'Now you can make your peace.' And it was not long before these two exchanged words of mutual forgiveness and affection.

In the lovely twin islands of Bernera and Boreray, which lie by North Uist, he also left his mark. In the latter his words were listened to by all except one man who churlishly continued sowing his seed while the preacher was sowing the seed of the Word. 'See,' he said, 'what this poor man is doing; but his work is all in vain.' And so it was. In the time of harvest nothing was reaped where this man had sown.

Across the water, beside 'Creag Hasda,' he preached in the open air. Giving out the opening verse of Psalm 65, he enlarged on the praise which the Lord would eternally obtain in His Zion which He redeemed. To this theme he spread his wings and soared with such freedom that the sun sank behind the blue waters of the Atlantic before he ended the service.

The writer laboured for four happy years in Glenmoriston where Finlay Munro's footprints—the story of which is well known—can be seen to this day. We are satisfied that this miracle cannot be explained in terms of natural events; but that we have in that quiet Highland wood, according to his own prediction, a visible memorial of a man whose word the Lord regarded. Living in a scientific and sceptical age, when 'we see not our signs' because 'there is no prophet,' we cannot hope to convince many that these and similar incidents witnessed to the verity of the Gospel preached by those men of God.

The First Ripe Sheaves.

AMONG the first fruits of harvest in Lewis was Angus Morrison, whose name we mentioned. He was a man of great mental powers and unabated zeal in the cause of the Lord.

Dr. John MacDonald, Ferintosh, had a special place in his affection. One late afternoon, as Angus was sitting in his father's house in South Dell, a woman, who had just returned from Stornoway, walked in. Angus asked for news from town. She had no news to give except that John MacDonald was expected to preach in the island the following day. This, however, was news which had the effect of transforming young Angus into something like a human arrow who travelled with all speed toward the spot where the Gospel was to be preached on the morrow. The day had already declined toward evening, but the joy in his heart made little of the long intervening moor and the gathering darkness. On the pathless heath, as he was well on the way, he heard what sounded like something or somebody falling into a bog. A shout from Angus elicited the information that the victim of the accident was none other than his dear friend, Malcolm MacRitchie, Uig, also on the same errand as himself. These two young men, thirsting for living waters, sat that day under the great preacher whose word fell on their souls like ' the dew on Hermon.'

Angus frequently visited the favoured shire of Caithness either as the guest of Mr. Finlay Cook, Reay, or following his calling as a fisherman. There he came in touch with such mighties as John MacIntosh, Farr, and Joseph MacKay, Strathhalladale. After that flashing genius, Alexander Gair, had passed from the scene he was appointed to preach to the Gaelic fishermen. This is an indication of how high a place he enjoyed in the esteem of the spiritual leaders of his day.

During one of the fishing seasons, Angus spent a happy Sabbath day in the company of a Caithness father who lived a fair distance inland. On the Monday he was very late in returning to his boat and crew. The rest of the fleet had put to sea hours before. His men complained that they had lost the day. Angus, full of cheer, however, set sail. Reaching a point not far from the shore, he cast his nets in the presence of a very dissatisfied crew. That day he landed an excellent catch, while those who toiled in deeper waters took but little. On subsequent occasions, when landings would happen to be light, his companions would say, ' It is time you visited again the old man at the hill.'

Among the young men who knew Angus well in his old age at Back were Mr. John MacLeod, latterly Principal of the Free Church College; Mr. George MacKay, late of Fearn, Ross-shire, and Mr. John R. MacKay, afterwards Professor of Greek in the Free Church College. On one occasion Mr. J. R. MacKay preached in the Back Church from the words, ' And the servant abideth not in the house for ever, but the son abideth ever.' It was a remarkable effort from so young a man. After the sermon, Mr. Hector Cameron, the minister, could not refrain from giving a public and characteristic indication of his delight at the young preacher's powers. Even then Mr. MacKay dwelt on the higher altitudes of theology. Many years afterwards a man who had listened to him that night at Back reminded him of the great freedom he then enjoyed. Mr. MacKay replied: ' Such freedom as I had that night I have not enjoyed since.' That such rising stars as these eagerly sought the company of Angus Morrison was the evidence of his own unconscious greatness as a Christian man.

A contemporary of Angus Morrison was the excellent Angus MacIver, Uig. He was a singer of incomparable sweetness and power. A person once listening to him ' putting out the line ' said, ' Such singing I cannot hope to hear on this side of Heaven.' If he excelled in praise he was also mighty in prayer. Even in public his eye was seldom dry as he pleaded with the Lord for a day of power. Catherine MacKay, Barvas, in what is decidedly her best song, speaks of him thus:

> ' Nach faca sibh bhraithrean,
>   Na bha aig' de lanachd na beath'?
>   'Nuair bhiodh e ag urnuigh,
>   Bhiodh silleadh o shuilean gu pailt;
>   Bhiodh e tagradh an comhmuidh
>   A chumhachd a dhoirteadh a mach
>   Air na peacaich bu thruagh,
>   Chum's gu faigheadh iad fuasgladh as.'

> (Brethren, saw not ye,
>   How much of life's fullness he enjoyed?
>   And how in supplication true,
>   His weeping eyes with tears would flow;
>   Always making earnest pleadings,
>   For the power to come down,
>   On the sinner in his bondage,
>   To be saved from God's just frown.)

When Angus MacIver was sent to serve as a Gaelic teacher to Argyll, he did not leave his prayers behind him. There, as was his wont, he sought out a secret place where he could call on the name of the Lord, free from external interruption. This he found among the rocks down by the sea. As a result of his wrestlings there he contracted a deep-seated asthmatic condition which made him fear that his days on earth were soon to end. He grieved especially at the thought of leaving a young wife and family unprotected and unprovided for in a world not always

kindly disposed towards the widow and the fatherless. This fear
weighed heavily on his spirit at the Throne of Grace. One day,
his wife noticed that ' the fashion of his countenance had altered,'
and enquired as to the cause of his unconcealed joy. ' The Lord,'
he said, ' gave me this day a promise that I would live to see
my children's children.' Many years afterwards when he was
at Back in Lewis, and in poor health, he was presented with
his first grandchild. To his wife who was present he said, ' This
is now the Word of the Lord fulfilled.' She, however, gave a
better exposition of the words by reminding him that the
promise was in the plural! From that illness he recovered and
he lived to see more than one grandchild.

During his stay at Maryburgh in Ross-shire there were some
whose souls were so richly nourished under his preaching that
they would pass other and more popular voices to enjoy what,
to them, was the finest of the wheat.

This good man passed away at Maryburgh, and is buried
at Fodderty. The beautiful experience associated with his death,
when, as some believed, an angel ministered to him, was a fit
end to a life devoted to God and His cause. His lonely and
godly wife shared in the blessing of that last hour.

Kenneth Ross, Lochs, was Angus MacIver's ' yokefellow '
in Argyll. He was sent to labour in Laga in the vicinity of
Strontian. When Kenneth arrived in the district his unbroken
rule that family worship must be kept wherever he lodged met
with stern opposition. As no one would agree to this invasion
of ancient domestic conduct Kenneth went his way. Walking
over the crest of the hill he was overtaken by a man named
Lachlan MacPherson, who pleaded with him to return to Laga
as he was willing to receive him into his home. With this man
Kenneth Ross stayed, and before he left the district he had the
joy of seeing three of Lachlan's sons converted. This happened
through his prayers at family worship. It appears that outside
that one home no one received lasting good through his labours.

As in the case of Gideon's fleece the blessing rested on the one family while the rest remained untouched by the dew of Heaven. This fact illustrates the force of the word which says, ' Be not forgetful to entertain strangers: for thereby some have entertained angels unawares.'

Kenneth Ross was a son of consolation who could often send ' the broken in heart ' away relieved. In Carloway, where he laboured for fourteen years, there was a man who had passed through a severe spiritual trial. He wondered in his own mind whether his trial was one which troubled any of God's people. A ' miserable comforter ' whom he consulted aggravated his condition by saying that, in his opinion, the trial he complained of could not enter into the experience of the Lord's people at all. In a state of alarm he visited Kenneth Ross. When he had finished his sad story Kenneth assured him that ' his sickness was not unto death.' ' The man you consulted,' Kenneth informed him, ' is one whom the Lord never drew very near to Himself, and whom, on the other hand, He never sent very far from Him.' These words describe the type of man who neither sinks very low nor soars very high, and whose spiritual sympathies are therefore limited.

Kenneth once passed through a subtle temptation himself. Loved by his flock at Carloway, he feared that ' all men spake well of him.' Therefore the ' woe ' resting on such rested on him. A friend in whom he confided on this point said: ' Mr. Ross, you may rest your mind, for I know of one who is very hard on you. Unlike those on whom such a woe does rest it is very seldom you speak well of *yourself*.' This judicious word was the means of scattering the cloud which troubled his mind, for Kenneth Ross was ever a companion of the man whose prayer was—' God be merciful to me a sinner.'

The huge Atlantic seas which almost incessantly surge on the western side of the Outer Hebrides can, in days of storm, be awe-inspiring. One stormy day as Kenneth Ross and his son watched the wind-driven waves breaking on the precipitous head of the ' Gallan ' at Uig he was alarmed to see a sailing vessel trying to navigate beyond the danger of this jutting rock. He earnestly prayed that God would send deliverance to the unknown ship. This He mercifully did.

Afterwards he visited the General Assembly meetings in Edinburgh. One day on the street a stranger stopped him and asked him who he was. It so happened that this man was the God-fearing captain of the vessel that Kenneth had seen from his native shore. The man told him how in his own prayers that day God gave him to see that another man was pleading on their behalf somewhere ashore. Assured that the Lord would answer their mutual prayers he encouraged his men. The vessel presently laboured out of its peril and reached calmer waters. The amazing story of how the Lord who ' sits on the floods ' heard his prayers that day filled Kenneth Ross with wonder, as did the experience of the unknown sailor.

A younger Christian than any of these was Donald Morrison, Fivepenny, Ness. He was only a lad of fifteen summers when he turned to the Lord through a tender personal appeal from Finlay Munro. In old age John MacRae would pay him the silent compliment of standing in the pulpit whenever he spoke at the Friday service. The kindly Murdo Stewart, catechist at Back, was his life-long companion. Donald arrived once at Back, and saw that Murdo Stewart was not in his accustomed place in Church. Afterwards when he called at his home he found him in a most disconsolate state, sighing out the woeful words: ' . . . a rod for the back of a fool.' Donald Morrison broke the snare by saying, ' Friend, these words are not for you. This is the word which I bring you from the Lord—" For your life is hid with Christ in God." ' This word indeed proved to be a leaf from the Tree of Life; and the meeting of praise and prayer which followed that day and that night was Murdo

Stewart's thankoffering to the One who had known his soul in adversity.

Donald used to tell of how as a young man he was present at a prayer meeting at Callernish. There lived in the district then a notable Christian woman known as 'Anna nighean an t'-saoir.' Annie had a frank way of telling young men what she thought of their public devotions, and Donald was apprehensive that if asked to engage in prayer he might afterwards suffer at her hands! After he had finished his prayer he saw her sitting behind him. Later, she took him by the hand and said, 'You began and finished as I prayed you would. Some weary us with too many words, and then we cease to pray with them. Then the prayer becomes unprofitable.' This advice helped Donald to become an apostle of brevity in all his public exercises.

The Rev. Peter MacLean, Stornoway, once had a visit from Donald Morrison accompanied by the well-known Annie MacLeod from Bayble. 'There is one beside you there, Donald,' said Mr. MacLean, 'and when I came home from Canada she had a sackful of godliness, but now you could put it all into the smallest vessel.' Donald defended his fair companion by reminding him that some good things had bulk and quantity to begin with, but as the process of refinement went on the quantity diminished and the quality improved. With this line of defence Mr. MacLean was well pleased.

Donald was once at Uig where, on a Friday, he listened to Donald MacLean, a worthy from Bragar. The Bragar Donald gave marks peculiar to the several kinds of religious deceivers within the professing Church of God. Among other choice things he said, 'There is no man in this large congregation who is more afraid of being deceived in his hope before God than I am. It is also my opinion that deceivers are of three kinds. There are the black, the speckled, and the white. With regard to the black one his iniquity and emptiness are before

the eyes of all, so that even a graceless world may see that
he is destitute of the grace of God. The other a graceless world
cannot know; but when he frequents the company of God's
people and attempts to share their experience and conversation
they can discern that he is but a stranger to the things of God.
The white one, however, may deceive both a graceless world
and the people of God. He is known only to the all-seeing
One. It is my great fear at times that it is to that last class
I myself belong.' In those times men did not take their eternal
salvation for granted.

The unconscious poetic instinct with which such almost
illiterate men could illustrate their spiritual experiences was often
a marked feature of their sayings. An island fisherman, once
speaking of the deep peace which possessed his heart when by
faith he found refuge and rest in Christ's Death and Righteousness, said, ' That day my peace was so great that I felt as if
the tiniest shell could float undisturbed on the western sea.'

Though approved in Christ, Donald Morrison often walked
under a cloud of sensible spiritual desertion. None could, therefore, be more tender than he in ministering comfort to the
mourner in Zion. Speaking once in the open air at Dell he
referred feelingly to the way poor believers often lost their
' receipt ' for what they had so carefully deposited in the heavenly
bank, and thinking that having lost this they had lost their all.
To such Christ would say, ' Though you have lost the " receipt "
your name is still in my Book and your treasure is safe in My
hands.' In other words the eternal salvation of the believer is
not dependent either on feeling or on an unclouded assurance,
but on Christ's faithfulness in the covenant which is ' ordered
in all things and sure.'

This excellent remark on the difference between faith and
feeling reminds one of another day in the North when, on a
communion Friday, a man asked for the evidences in the life
of those who make their calling and election sure. Some of

the speakers found the subject a great deep. The day, however, was redeemed by a pensioned soldier who said that although he had never seen with his own eyes his name in ' the big book in London ' he knew it was there since the king's money came to hand with unfailing regularity. In the same way he knew also his name to be in the Book of Life among the elect of God since the Lord, from the day He called him by His Spirit, continued to nourish his soul out of Christ's unsearchable fulness.

Donald had his trials as well as his consolations. To a friend he once said, ' I have had three weeks in heaven.' ' In that case,' replied his friend, ' you may now expect three weeks in a state opposite to that.' He knew night and day.

Late in life, when his bodily vigour had abated, he would walk once more the long distance between Ness and Uig. On the way he was overtaken by his friend, Mr. John MacRae. Mr. MacRae affectionately upbraided him, an old man, for venturing so far from home. Asking Donald whether to hear the Gospel was his chief motive in attending the communion at Uig, he said, ' To be honest, Mr. MacRae, no. My reason for coming so far is that I may have some further converse there with my friends in the Lord before I leave the world.' To this confession, Mr. MacRae replied, ' I have always held you in high esteem, Donald; but I never thought more of you than I do today.'

No man in his day ordered his life more in keeping with God's Word than Donald Morrison. Once in illustrating his dependence on the Word of God as his lamp and guide he told how once in a mist at sea he lost sight of land, as well as all sense of direction. When the mist cleared he saw he was a long way from the shore and moving in the wrong direction. Without the light of the Word he could not, in other words, find his way to the Home above, or keep his feet in the straight path.

The colourful and attractive John MacDonald—known locally as Iain Buidhe—from North Tolsta, was Donald Morrison's friend. John was a charming speaker, whose pictorial and sanctified mind could draw spiritual lessons from the world of nature. He lived where he could see the western sea in its fierce and gentle moods. ' When I see a winter calm, with the sea lapping at the base of the cliff, I am not deceived. I know a storm is on the way. So it is with me in this life: my moments of calm are often followed by storms of temptation and trial.'

The sea, with all its ancient terrors, often furnished those good men with illustrations of the spiritual life. Those who do business in great waters see the wonders of the Lord. In this connection a friend of John used to tell a story of a stormy day at sea. They were driven by a rough wind towards a high precipitous headland which jutted far into the sea. ' In that headland we saw our impending doom; but we also knew that on its sheltered side there was safety and a calm sea.

' In the same way God's Justice, like a great mountain towering in a sea of wrath, threatens our destruction. But once we shelter in Christ as our Righteousness, God's Justice and all the attributes of the Eternal shelter us and stand between us and the wrath to come.'

The island custom of marking sheep for purposes of identification he made use of to illustrate the doctrines of election and regeneration. God, he once said, had revealed to him that when He made choice of him in Christ He marked him with the blue stone of electing love; and with the red He sealed him in the day of regeneration when on his conscience He sprinkled the blood of Christ.

Sometimes John worked in town. Up among the rafters in a big shed, amid noise and danger, he once saw a mother dove building its nest and caring for its young till they were able to fly away. By this lovely figure he spoke of how the Church of God could not only survive in a world of strife and enmity, but also nourish and protect her seed till God took them away to Himself.

John was once the means, under God, of preventing a grave local disaster. A number of fishermen in the act of leaving the shore he solemnly warned to stay in port as, he feared, the deceptive day was laden with death for some. The men, awed by his seriousness, obeyed him. But in the next village, eight miles away, some who ventured to sea that day perished in the storm.

There was another man on the west side of the island of whom so much is still remembered that it is unnecessary to say anything here beyond giving a few unrecorded incidents from his life. I refer to Malcolm MacLean, Shawbost.

A man of almost unceasing prayer, and deeply exercised as a believer, he was no stranger to the sore trials which attend the Christian life. Passing once through a season of ' manifold temptations ' he sank helplessly in his spirits. When his attached friend, John MacIver, came to see him he was earnestly asked by Malcolm to remember him at the Throne of Grace, and to bring back whatever word the Lord was pleased to send. When after a few days John made his way with ' good tidings ' to his home he found Malcolm helping his wife in her domestic task by plying a butter churn. It hardly moved in his discouraged hand. John MacIver quoted the word which the Lord had sent to relieve this weary saint: ' And the God of peace shall bruise Satan under your feet shortly.' The effect was immediate. The handle which hardly moved in his hand a moment before he now plied with such vigour that the bottom of the churn gave way, and the cream spread out on the floor. If his good wife was annoyed that night this tried man of God had his hour of needed comfort.

There was a young man from Barvas who used to tell of one of his first attempts at public prayer. Since he was a mere boy and very hesitant, Malcolm, in a spirit of tender sympathy and love, would support him with a brief but audible prayer of his own. ' Lord, help the child,' he repeated several times. And help did come from above: so much so that the aged saint had to change his petition into praise. ' Praise be to Thee for having helped the child,' he exclaimed as ' the child ' was about halfway through his own prayer.

This young man was Murdo MacLeod, who afterwards settled at Swainbost. Murdo himself was a quaint, eccentric man. In his public prayers he was seldom direct. Almost invariably he presented his petitions in the form of an imaginary dialogue in which the parties concerned were sometimes the Lord and the Adversary, sin and grace, or the old man and the new man of the heart. If the worthy man sometimes lost his bearings as he pitted the one against the other in hot opposition it was obvious to all on what side he wished to be.

Malcolm MacLean was present once at a cottage meeting in Shader. He was given the Bible to conduct family worship. As he took the Book in his hand he cried out, ' Satan, Satan, Satan, leave this company! ' He then handed the Bible to an elder present saying, ' All is well now; he shall not trouble us more tonight.' The sense of great peace which fell on the spirits of the worshipping company made that night memorable.

The neighbouring islands of Skye and Harris were equally favoured by the Lord. There are two names, especially, which have a unique place in our evangelical literature. They are the names of men who were, at least, of stature equal to that of any we have mentioned. In Skye, Donald Munro was supreme among his contemporaries. This remarkable man, who died in 1830, at the age of 57, lost the use of his eyes when a lad of fourteen years. If his great mental powers were clouded by a Miltonic affliction, he was, unlike the great Puritan poet, forced by extreme poverty, to earn his living by way of providing the music which accompanied the nocturnal revellings of his fellow

islanders. On account of his native eloquence, and the ease
with which he mastered the letter of the Bible, he united to his
musical attainments the office of catechist. Neither the 'blind
shepherds' who appointed him, nor Donald himself, saw anything ludicrous in the doubly blind fiddler being also the spiritual
monitor to the community. When the evangelical doctrine at
last dispelled the prevailing darkness, Donald was among the
first whom God called into His grace. The new doctrine was
not popular. One man exhorted his fellows not to be taken in
with such preaching 'for if it is true, every one of us has the
devil behind our back door!' The light which Donald Munro
now enjoyed on the Word of God was a source of amazement
to all who heard him. His wonderful insight into its unsearchable
riches was only equal to his prayers. These were Spurgeonic
in their directness, reverence, holy intimacy, and melting effect.
The Rev. John MacRae, no mean judge, said once that a godlier
man he had never seen in this world. For the same reason,
the gifted John Morrison of Harris would weep as he spoke of
his heavenly unction. It was a remarkable coincidence that
Murdo MacDonald, his spiritual counterpart in Lewis, died in
Donald Munro's arms. Their bones rest in the same grave,
beside a fern-kissed stream, almost in the shadow of the Coolin
hills.

Like Donald Munro, the above mentioned John Morrison,
Harris, is so well known through his songs, that little can be
added to his fame. Dr. Henderson has done well in giving us
his poems in such fulness, but the biographical sketch provided
is meagre and defective. Besides, the spirit of the man is hardly
understood. Morrison was a poet of great depth, vitality and
inimitable imagery. The primitive freshness of some of his
verses is their most marked quality. Many of his verses have
an indescribable, unsullied beauty. His marvellous skill in opening windows which let us see better into the eternal world is
without compare.

He is equally fascinating in his delineation of the Christian as a complex man, in whom grace reigns, but against whom iniquities prevail. This insight was not of his own vision, but was the result of great gifts of mind, richly anointed by the Spirit of God. The greatest compliment ever paid to John Morrison was by Dr. John MacDonald, who said on a Friday of a communion, after listening to the ' Men ' present, ' I know a blacksmith in Harris, who knows more theology than you all.' This was the evaluation of a man who knew all the ' men of renown ' in his own generation.

Elect Ladies.

IN the feminine circle of those who adorned the doctrine of the Lord there were in the North 'elect ladies' of outstanding eminence. One could mention the names of Peggy MacKenzie, Stornoway; Catherine MacKay, Barvas; Annie Campbell, Point; Mrs. MacFarquhar, Ness; Margaret MacKenzie, North Tolsta, and Christina MacDonald, Soay.

Peggy MacKenzie was an affectionate but transparent Christian who would in no wise conceal that her lines had fallen in pleasant places. She was an attached friend of Murdo MacDonald, Bayhead—a lone star in the evangelical firmament long before the reviving breath of the Lord had swept over the land. Some have spoken of Murdo MacDonald as an awakening voice which hailed the dayspring from on high. He was certainly a swift witness against 'the dumb dogs' who sat content in the stifling atmosphere of the deadening formalism which everywhere prevailed. In secret he was a prince with God; and the grace which so richly rested on his life earned him the honourable name of 'Great Murdo of the graces.' His spiritual stature may be realised when Finlay Cook compared him favourably with the excellent John Grant of Strathy, Sutherland. In the Isle of Skye, as we have seen, he found such a congenial companion in the godly Donald Munro that they made a covenant to 'sleep in the same grave' that they might 'arise together in the morning.' One of his public remarks will go to show how he lived as a consecrated Christian: 'There is not a day but I bring myself before the Lord in His Word; and when the Word discovers the sins of my life and thought I resort to the fountain of blood, where my sins are covered and washed away.' But this by the way.

Peggy MacKenzie once administered a public rebuke in Stornoway for the cold reception the people had given to a band of choice young men from Skye who had come to the communion services. When she afterwards appeared at her own home with one of them a friend said, ' What, Peggy, if you are bringing home a betrayer? ' ' If so,' she replied, ' the loss will be his and not ours.' When the company sat down to dine she asked a blessing in these words, ' No man ever called Thee a hard Master, but such as knew Thee not.'

Her friend, Catherine MacKay, was of the mercurial type—light and shade would pass over her soul in quick succession. We think it was she who on one occasion repeated the words: ' If I were told that only two out of this generation were to go to heaven I should hope to be one; and if I were told that only two were to be lost, I should fear to be one of these.' President J. Edwards once expressed himself in similar words. This tremendous spiritual earnestness was a characteristic of the older Highland Christians. Catherine's saying recalls an incident which once took place on a Hebridean moor. It throws light on how fear and hope may alternate in the life of an exercised believer. A man once crossing a lone moor became interested in the rather strange behaviour of a person some distance ahead of him. At times he would run; at times he would stand still. Overtaken in the way by the other he was asked why he acted so strangely. He answered, ' When I thought of myself as on the way to heaven I could not but run; but when fear possessed me that I might be on the way to a lost eternity, I could not but stand still.'

Catherine's spiritual affection for that choice Christian, John MacKay, Barvas, was deep and constant. In one of her darker moods she once expressed the pathetic wish that if the Lord

had decreed to shut her out of heaven she might be allowed
the favour of ' a little window ' through which she could look
up at John MacKay in his happiness! She often questioned
her own interest in Christ, but never his. In her poems she
gives John the palm among the worthies of her time. This
good man went to Canada at a comparatively early age; but
Catherine and he held such near communion in the Lord that
on the day he died she at once became aware of the fact. And
there was no literary communication between them throughout
those years of separation.

Her faith in the promises of God as they stand related to
the spiritual and temporal needs of His people led her to the
Throne of Grace with every need. Anxious to attend a communion in a distant parish she once prayed for suitable footwear.
Her secret place of prayer was a small sheltered hollow on
the moor. It so happened that a visitor was on the moor that
day in pursuit of lawful game. Seeing something in motion
above the ground, and mistaking it for something wild, he fired
his shot. This was nothing more than Catherine's bonnetted
head moving to and fro in devotional earnestness. Getting an
interpreted account of what brought her there to pray he
extended his apologies along with a gift of gold—more than
enough to buy her shoes.

' What a quick translation to heaven if I had been killed
here! ' she remarked to the astonished and much-relieved men.

Catherine was also remarkable for her voice. When she
dovetailed her nightingale notes into the last bar of the precentor's ' line ' it seemed to many like a melody from the vestibule
of heaven.

A brief sketch of this notable woman, along with several
of her poems, was given in 1927 by the Rev. Alexander MacRae,
Kintail and Tongue, whose forbear, ' Mr. William ' of Barvas,
Catherine admired as the poor man's friend.

On a Sabbath morning in the year 1871 Catherine MacKay
lay dying. To those who asked her if she wished to be remembered in the prayers of the congregation she answered, ' Intercession is being made for me above.'

There was in the Isle of Skye a Christian lady who much
resembled Catherine MacKay. She was Christina Macdonald,
who lived in Soay—a minute isle on the coast of Skye. The
famed minister of Snizort, Mr. Roderick MacLeod, gave her
the lovely name of ' Queen of Soay.' And this was how it
happened. During a season of communion Mr. MacLeod saw
her walking toward the manse bringing gifts for Mrs. MacLeod's
hospitable table. Looking at her wistfully in the distance he
said, ' I see the Queen of Soay coming bearing there burdens:
one, a burden of sin; another, a burden of grace; and another,
a burden of the good things of this life for ourselves.' This
surely was a happy comment on one whose life was enriched
by the superlative graces of faith, hope and love.

A word from Mr. Murdoch MacAskill, Dingwall, in a
sermon which he preached in Urquhart reveals how Christina
stood in the eyes of her Christian friends. ' Two of the most
godly persons I have ever known,' he said, ' were Dr. John
Kennedy and a girl in the Isle of Soay. They had two things
in common, though neither of them could tell which of these
two things affected them most—the sight they both obtained
of their own lost state as sinners, or the view they enjoyed of
the love of the Saviour.'

Mr. Nicol Nicolson, who admired her Christian bearing,
used to say that the heavenliness which sat on her face, like a
ray of light, was a benediction equal to her conversation. At
her funeral service Mr. Nicolson dwelt tenderly on the words—
' The king's daughter is all glorious within.' This gracious
woman confessed the Lord at the age of fifteen years, and till
she died at the age of ninety she adorned her profession. In
the place where she lived and prayed the fragrance of her

Christian life lingered long after she was gathered home. We are not sure whether the Lewis Catherine ever met the Skye Christina, but if those two ever did meet they would each have seen reflected in one another, like Mercy and Christiana, the unconscious image of their Lord.

Not far from where Catherine MacKay lived there was another excellent young woman, Gormelia MacLean by name. Gormelia used to tell of how she and others once went down to the shore to cut seaweed. As the tide had not ebbed sufficiently when they arrived, they used the spare hour in sorting some potato pits near the shore. Meantime, and for some reason unknown to her, she felt she ought to visit the home of Malcolm Campbell, Bragar. Arriving at Malcolm's house she found him engaged in prayer with his friend, John Smith. Gormelia's arrival was literally an answer to their prayer. They both welcomed her with the words—'Blessed be thou of the Lord who has come to our help in our old age.'

It happened that a few days before the local minister, Mr. N. MacArthur, had given Malcolm a gift of half a crown. It happened also that very morning that Malcolm had a dream. In his dream a dying Christian woman from a distant village appeared to him and asked him for half a crown. Gormelia, therefore, appeared also at the opportune moment that she might, in answer to the prayers of those two men, carry the gift where it was so urgently needed.

On receiving the coin the dying woman said, 'I am going Home, but I owe the merchant half a crown, and I have been earnestly asking the Lord to send me this money to discharge my debt before I left the world.'

A story similar to this used to be told of a good woman who lived in Glenurquhart. This lady happened to be in temporal straits. She prayed earnestly to the Great Provider to send her the promised daily bread. Several times she thought of telling the well known Alexander Fraser of her plight, but

each time her courage failed her. One evening on the way to
a service she was surprised to see Alexander waiting for her.
Pointing to a corner of the dyke, he said with characteristic
abruptness, 'Here is your meal, and instead of keeping me
awake in the night again come and ask for it.'

Another name we would mention is that of a lady who
belonged to a later generation. She was a native of Ness and
her name was Margaret MacIver. Margaret began to seek
the good part when she was about twelve years of age. Already
sensible of a strong attachment to God's people and God's
house she would wait on the Lord in the public means of grace
while her quickened soul drank at the Fountain of Life. Sometimes in passing out with the worshipping congregation some
would affectionately pat her head saying: 'Is this the child
who is seeking the Lord?'

Margaret, who was born abont 1850, was still very young
when she had a curious dream which made a deep impression
on her mind. She saw in her dream that the resurrection morning had come. She saw herself arising out of the grave to
welcome her glorious Redeemer. The vision was so vivid that
she retained its imagery all her life. Afterwards when she
settled down as a young married woman at North Tolsta she
recognised the place which she had seen in her dream—a green
bank decked by a variety of wild flowers, and near which the
restless waves spend themselves on a golden strand. More than
seventy years afterwards her body was laid to rest in that very
spot.

When she grew up she made it a matter of prayer that
if the Lord had ordained a husband for her He would provide
her with a companion who feared and loved Himself. Her
prayer was heard. Her home in North Tolsta was afterwards
known as 'Bethel' to those who, on the way to ordinances,
tarried there for a night.

The grace which so richly rested on Margaret MacKenzie, as she was now known, was seen in her constant watchfulness over her own heart, lips, and daily conduct. In mixed company she was careful not to debase Christian conversation. If the Spirit moved her to leave a word in season she would do so without hesitation. To a young Christian who once visited her she counselled: ' Be sure that you acknowledge the Lord in all your ways, and He will direct your paths. Pray especially for a bridled tongue, for it is an ensnaring member. Never unbosom yourself unwisely, and pray much when you are in the company of others that you may not be damaged by your own words. You will be surprised to find that you may feel more devoted to some of God's people of whom you know little, and that your heart will open out to some who are not yet Christians more than to some who profess to be. Eternity alone will reveal why this is so. Ask the Lord to enable you to pray in the Spirit. Only in prayer do we enjoy true nearness to Him and taste of His love. Hide nothing from Him, and the more He shows you of your sins and sinfulness the more you will thank Him. Whatever you do take Him always at His Word.'

The exhortation embodied in this last sentence was the secret of what to some was Margaret's prophetic spirit. In every difficulty she asked counsel of the Lord. When He sent His Word, however much it might seem to be in conflict with present appearances, she never doubted the issue. This is where her faith excelled. Many instances could be given of how she enjoyed the secret of the Lord in impersonal matters affecting even nations and men.

In her prayers she invariably made mention of kings and those in authority that God would give them wisdom to rule in His fear and in righteousness. When George the Fifth died she told her friends that his eldest son would never sit on his father's throne. Urged to explain her incredible statement she replied: 'Who is he that saith, and it cometh to pass, when the Lord commandeth it not?' (Lam. iii. 37). Unable to read the English language she was not familiar with royal names. One day she asked if the king's next son had a daughter. On being told that he had, she said, 'Pray for that little girl. She is to carry a heavy burden and live in very distressing times.'

The measure of her Christian charity may be inferred from the following incident. A neighbouring minister belonging to another denomination once called to see her. When he apologised for bearing a different ecclesiastical name to her own she said in a homely parable, 'A good woman once married a man who had been married before and who had a family. Loving her husband she loved his children too; for although they were not hers she saw his likeness in them, and that fact knit them to her heart. You belong not to my Church, but every one in whom I see the image of God to that person my heart is knit in Christ.' Nothing gave her greater happiness than Christian fellowship. She was one day in her home with a friend engaged in conversation 'which concerned the King.' A man walked in who introduced a different note into their talk. She instantly rebuked him saying, 'Here we were reposing in the shade of a pleasant gourd, but your words have acted as worms to destroy it all.'

Someone asked her to explain the request of the foolish virgins when they said to the wise—'Give us of your oil.' She replied, 'Did you ever hear of godless persons on their death bed asking the Lord's people to pray for them? Well, that is the meaning of their cry.'

One of the beautiful things in the life of this good woman was that of a covenant which she made with two of her Christian friends. As these three were one day working together they enjoyed a large measure of 'the blessing that maketh rich.' While under the power of this shower of love they promised each other that whatever trials the Lord would send them they would bear one another's burdens in prayer and practical sympathy. This lovely bond was broken only in death.

As a mother, God gave her the reward of a mother's prayers. When her first child was born she became seriously ill. In that hour, however, when her life was hanging on a slender thread, the words, ' A seed shall come and do service to Him,' supported her. She was raised up. Afterwards she was given a fuller assurance with regard to her family: ' And all thy children shall be taught of the Lord, and great shall be the peace of thy children.' She lived to see all her family resting in the hope of salvation.

The day her like-minded husband passed away he sat listening to the conversation of Christian friends. A humble man of few words all he could say was, ' I often thanked the Lord that His Kingdom is not in word but in power.' His wife said in reply, ' You take that as your staff over this Jordan.' It was her last word of comfort to her dearest earthly friend. Before many hours had passed he had crossed that stream, on the nearer bank of which rests the shadow of death, but the farther side of which, for God's people, is bright with the light of an endless day.

An event which signified her own departure was the birth of her last grandchild. The day that happened she said, ' This tells me that my prolonged life is coming to an end, for He promised me " Peace " when I should see my children's children.'

Fourteen days before the end a friend found her weeping quietly alone. She said, ' Today my thoughts are down in the place where my bones shall lie till the last trump shall sound. My soul is already in eternity, and the only obstacle between me and the full enjoyment of God is this frail body.' It was on a lovely morning in June, 1940, as the sun was rising, that her soul joined ' the spirits of just men made perfect.'

Margaret MacKenzie had a young relative who devoted himself to the ministry of the Gospel. When young John arrived home from the south after his conversion his godly and gifted father would have him engage in prayer at family worship. His parent was anxious to know if the boy had really undergone a saving change, and this he would judge by the nature of his prayer. ' Before the prayer ended,' as his father said afterward, ' I knew John had grace, but listening to him I was afraid I had none myself.' This promising young man was killed in the first world war.

'These Called on God.'

THE Evangelical Revival in the Highlands brought into being a Church which knew the way to The Throne of Grace and whose prayers ascended up to heaven 'like pillars of smoke.' It was a Church which travailed for the rebirth of souls, and for the upbuilding of God's Zion. And God made her a joyful mother of children.

One precious fruit of the Revival was the institution of the family altar. Worship in the family became almost a universal practice in all those places where the Lord had made known His power. It is sad to think that this invaluable act of devotion is now a mere memory in many homes and communities.

There was a district in the North where for over two miles the homes of the people, mostly crofters, lay hard by the wayside. On a calm evening along the whole of that road, the one neighbour might hear the other singing a psalm at the hour of family worship.

Dr. John Kennedy once referred to the decline which the devotional life of the Church had suffered within his own recollection. The former generation of Christians not only prayed, but would continue to wait on the Lord till the answer came. They looked for the return of their prayers. In his own latter days, men were praying as formerly, but the old fervent spirit of importunity had largely passed away.

A younger Ross-shire minister than Dr. Kennedy used to quote one of the 'Men' who once illustrated the meaning of persevering prayer. A piper, he said, went round the doors playing his tunes. Those who did not appreciate his music, and who would have him depart, would throw him a coin before he had hardly begun. At a certain door, however, though he played all his tunes as best he could, no one seemed to hear. At last, when he was about to leave, the door opened. ' I like your music, and I wanted to hear your tunes to the end; otherwise I would have rewarded you sooner,' said the kindly person who opened the door. The Lord, in other words, takes great delight in the prayers of His people, and His delays are not to be taken for denials. Jacob got the blessing not immediately, but at the break of day after a long night of wrestling with the Angel. Paul also was long on his knees before the Lord opened the door and blessed him with the needed grace for the conflict.

Our mentioning Paul's prayer reminds one of a noted High-land woman who was once oppressed with a heavy temptation. In answer to her cry for help the words—' My grace is sufficient for thee,' came seasonably to her trembling spirit. But no sooner was the snare broken than the enemy assailed her again by insinuating that the words from which she derived such comfort were meant for Paul alone. Again she went to the Lord in prayer, and again He graciously delivered her in the great promise of Psalm 105: ' The word which he commanded to a thousand generations.' The happy light then broke in upon her mind that the word which came from Heaven to Paul in his day of trouble was appointed to strengthen and reassure untold thousands of God's afflicted people to the end of time.

In those days of restricted communication, prayer was often the living link by which absent friends could still enjoy fellow-ship in the Lord. The Spirit of the Lord, who dwells in the heart, is infinite, and in this way He can draw together the dispersed members of God's family.

A lovely story may be told of how ' The Communion of Saints ' becomes a wonderful reality through mutual prayer. Two young men from the North once covenanted to pray for one another at a set time each day.

In the course of time the two lads went their separate ways. One returned to his home in Lewis, and the other left for the Antipodes. Each day after the mid-day meal, they were to remember one another in prayer. Unversed in the laws of astronomy, and unaware, at the time, of how night and day would change through the distance between them, the result was that the prayers of the one who remained at home would touch his friend in Australia at midnight, while the prayers of the lad who lived on the other side of the world would, in like manner, touch and refresh his friend in the far away Hebrides.

There was another young Ross-shire man who emigrated to Canada. There he toiled for many years without much regard for the wholesome spiritual influences by which he was sur- rounded in the days of his youth. After a time he ailed and had to lie in bed. There his mind went back to other days. In the panorama of memory he could see himself again in the Church at Ferintosh. The minister was in the pulpit, and he could even recall the text and fragments of the sermon. As the whole scene presented itself to his mind he was deeply affected by the recollection. So much so that he was led to pray that God would visit him with His salvation. From that experience a new man in Christ came into being. The word which had lain so long in fallow ground, had taken root. The faithful praying minister of his boyhood days had gone Home, but he was still speaking in the memory of one of his people, and his prayers were still being answered. It is a story which should encourage every herald of salvation who may be tempted to think that their earnest labour is in vain.

There were some whose secret prayers did not always remain a secret. Angus Young of Kilmallie, for example, would at times take to one of the hills overlooking Loch Eil, and there, unconscious of the power of his voice, and the way in which sound carries better over a calm sheet of water, he would pour out his soul before God. There were seasons when his earnest voice could be heard by those who lived across the Loch. Such men were once the glory of the land.

Later on we shall mention the refreshing brevity of some of the ' Men's ' public prayers. Let me, however, give an instance of how a praying man, in the enjoyment of spiritual freedom, could forget time altogether. A worthy man in Lochcarron was on one occasion reminded by his young daughter of the unusual length of one of his public prayers. He quietly answered her: ' My dear, when you are speaking to a Person you love much, you are apt to forget the time.' This was the excellent Duncan MacLean.

On a Communion Sabbath in the North, the felt presence of the Lord was so overpowering that the presiding minister found it difficult to speak. Many were melted down, for a ' bright cloud had overshadowed them.' Some time afterwards, a good man who was present, remarked in his prayer how at the dedication of Solomon's temple, ' the priest could not stand to minister because of the cloud, for the glory of the Lord had filled the house of the Lord.' That remarkable prayer ended with the words: ' As we now descend from the Mount give us grace that the tables of the law may not be found broken in our hands.'

Pride and Self were two heart evils against which those men employed all their spiritual weapons, and especially the weapon of ' All Prayer.' One much tried man was once heard pleading with the Lord that He might ' hold him up.' But before he had gone very far with his plea, it came into his mind that he should also ask the Lord to hold him down as well!

This fear of sin reminds us of a man who once set off to pray that the Lord, in a time of drought, might send rain on the earth. It was a warm summer day, and his secret place of prayer was on the top of a little hill clothed with trees. Arriving at his trysting place, and feeling weary, he lay down to rest. Immediately he fell asleep. He awoke with the sound of rain among the thick, leafy boughs which overshadowed him. There and then he blessed the Lord for sending refreshing rain, and for sending it before he had prayed. Had it come after his prayer he might have ascribed the given favour to the efficacy of his own prayer, and not to God's mercy alone.

Indwelling sin in all its manifestations those men always spoke of as "the old man." It was the hated and hurtful burden which clung to them to the end. Their growth in grace and holiness advanced in the measure in which sin became more oppressive and more exceeding sinful. The well-known John MacKenzie of Gairloch ("Ceisdear Mór Mhealbhaig") was once asked by Principal John MacLeod as to how he was. 'I am,' said John, 'an old man carrying an old man.'

An impressive instance of how experience may teach the believer, and how greater light in the mind and greater tenderness in the conscience may affect his public devotions may be mentioned. It was a remark made by Roderick MacIver, Ness, Lewis, in one of his last public prayers: 'Lord thou knowest that we cannot now mention in secret before Thyself what we could once mention in the hearing of our fellow men.'

The prayers of those good men did not always ring with the note of cloudless assurance or permanent spiritual comfort. There was an excellent Christian girl in the Highlands who, in the first flush of her young but untried Christian love, took upon herself to rebuke two good men to whom she had listened at a prayer meeting. In broken accents they had each bewailed 'the years which the locusts had eaten,' and she could not then understand the cause of their spiritual dejection.

Later in the day she spoke to them about their woeful utterances. On hearing what she said one of the men wept and quoted the words of the Prophet: 'The people of thy holiness have possessed it but a little while' (Is. 63: 18). The words were meant to convey how little he had enjoyed the fellowship and the love of the Lord, and how sin and Satan had cast a blight over his soul.

Mary Smith, of Ness, lived to understand why Roderick MacIver mentioned above and Donald MacDonald had prayed that day out of a broken heart.

A custom which involved much self denial, but which is now passing away, was that of meeting for prayer in the early morning. Mary Cameron, a young Christian girl from Tobermory in Mull, was so anxious to attend the morning prayer meeting that she misread the hands of the clock. Dressing hurriedly, she ran toward the Church. No one had arrived. She returned home greatly wondering and sad at heart. But as she entered her home, she saw that it was not seven o'clock, but half-past one in the morning. Mary was a convert of Christopher Munro, and to the end she carried the peculiar fragrance which followed the ministry of that gentle and holy servant of Christ.

The shadow of poverty which so often rested on the homes of some of those who were rich in faith, helped to deepen their dependence on the Lord. It brought them to see the faithfulness of him who never fails to provide. Donald MacKay, Lewis, was a poor but godly man. One morning he was told by his sister than there was nothing in the house for breakfast. ' Joseph's storehouses are full,' was Donald's hopeful answer. After prayer and worship, he went forth to bring home peat fuel. He lifted a peat and under it lay half-a-crown. He lifted another with the same surprising result. Some time before a man happened to be passing this spot on the moor. He knew the peats belonged to Donald MacKay. The thought came into his mind that he should leave the two coins where he would be sure to find them. And there they lay against the day of need.

Another remarkable instance of God's over-ruling providence in providing for the needs of His people may be mentioned. In the island of Scalpay in Harris there was a good man on whose mind the words of the wise man fastened themselves with peculiar insistence: ' Cast thy bread upon the waters, for thou shalt find it after many days.' Looking at his store of meal it occurred to him one day that he should half-fill a watertight barrel with meal and cast it into the sea! This he did.

Months afterwards men from the remote island of St. Kilda visited Harris. In course of conversation they mentioned how the winter and spring storms had prevented the usual ship from calling with provisions, and how they would have suffered hunger had not a barrel of excellent meal landed on their shore.

This story used to be told by Mr. Matheson, who laboured for some years in Scalpay as lay preacher.

How God rewards the prayer of faith was once illustrated at a fellowship meeting by one of the 'Men.' A good woman in the district found herself one day with nothing in her home to sustain her bodily life. She pleaded earnestly in prayer that the Lord might send her a morsel of bread. At that moment two lads happened to be passing her door carrying a supply of bread to a local shop. Hearing her earnest voice in prayer they listened. ' Come,' said the one to his fellow, ' and let us drop one of these through the window.' This they did, having decided to pay for it themselves. As she was in the act of praising the Great Giver for his seasonable mercy, one of the lads walked in and said: ' It was not the Lord who sent it—we dropped it in.' ' Oh, my dear,' she said, ' Satan himself might have come with it, but it was the Lord who sent it.'

A lovely story of answered prayer used to be told of a noted woman in the island of Arran, whose unconverted husband was dying. One day shortly before he died she arrived at Church as her minister, Mr. MacNicol, was giving out the text. It was the words of Queen Esther: ' Let my life be given me at my petition, and my people at my request.' As she stood behind the door, an unseen listener, her soul went up to God on behalf of her husband. ' O Lord,' she wept, ' my husband's soul at my request.' Her prayer was heard. A few days afterwards, coming in from the place of her secret devotions, she addressed him affectionately: ' Tomorrow at this hour you will be singing the praises of the Redeemer in Heaven.' He passed away at the hour she said, resting on the merits of Christ, and rejoicing in the hope of the glory of God.

In concluding this chapter, I shall relate two anecdotes which show that when the godly Highlander left his native heath, he did not leave his praying behind him.

During the American Civil War, a Highland soldier was once brought before his commanding officer for being, as his accusers thought, in communication with the enemy under cover of night. At the interview with his superiors, the man explained that he was only praying to God, and not conversing with men. The commander—a shrewd man, and familiar with his Bible— after he had carefully examined him, said: ' Let us hear you pray now, for never had you more need of prayer.' The pious Highlander, there and then, fell on his knees and addressed his Maker in reverent and Scriptural language. His prayer revealed that not only was he familiar with the Word of God, but was, as a true believer, deeply exercised in his spirit. When he had finished the officer said: ' You may go. No one could have prayed so, without long apprenticeship. Those who have never attended drill, fare but ill at a review.'

More favoured than this misunderstood Highlander was a band of Hebridean sailors who served in the same ship. Every day at a convenient hour, they met to pray together. The captain of the ship was a Christian man. He overheard them one day as they were singing part of Psalm 45, where mention is made of the King's daughter who is all-glorious within. Afterwards, he spoke to them about the peculiar glory of the Church as the daughter of God and the Bride of Christ, and whose garments of Righteousness and Salvation were purchased and prepared by the obedience and death of her Lord.

We mentioned another fruit of the Evangelical revival. It was that exquisite Psalm singing which had such an effect on the emotions, and such a sanctifying influence on the Lord's people. The latent gift of song when it became articulate under the touch of the Divine power was, without controversy, a sublime thing. Nothing like it was ever heard in the land before. It was something new and heavenly. When God's spirit, like a gale from the Eternal hills swept over the singing multitudes, the effect was indescribable. Listening strangers who knew neither the people nor their language invariably had but one comparison to make. It was like the notes of a great and unutterably moving Æolian harp. The people sang for joy, for the shout of a King was among them. The unique manner in which one could listen to the individual voice of the precentor on the one hand, and to the multitude on the other, helped to deepen the impression made. For a man to lead the thousands present, he needed grace in his heart, affection for the people, spiritual sympathy with the words sung, and a voice that would do justice to the occasion.

Stories could be told of how sometimes the singing affected those who heard it. Three Hebridean fishermen were once travelling across the lonely Sutherlandshire moor on the way home from the east coast. With the approach of night they decided to seek rest and shelter at the first dwelling house by the way. The timid woman who came to the door at which they knocked refused them even the shelter of the barn. Assuring her, however, that they were upright men, they quietly took possession of it. At worship before they lay down to rest one of the men said to a companion who had a voice of rare melody and power, ' Come, sing this psalm; and if ever you extracted music from *Martyrdom* do so now.'

Meantime, the man of the house came home, and as he was preparing to remove the intruders the sweet cadences of a psalm fell on his ear. With an anxious look on his face he turned to his wife and said, 'Angels have visited us, and we refused to take them in.' In a few moments the men were brought in to share in the warmth and hospitality of their home.

Only when touched by Divine grace did the tongue of the dumb sing. Malcolm MacArthur, a young man from Lewis, awoke one morning to find that he could sing in a new way. The previous night he had tasted that the Lord was gracious. No one who heard his voice could forget its moving melody and sweetness.

One of the great Gaelic leaders of praise was Christopher MacRae of Lochalsh. Christopher, with his magnificent tenor voice, captivated the ears of his generation. There were others, like Alexander MacLeod of Fivepenny—afterwards minister of Coigeach—who were pre-eminent in their generation. Occasionally leaders of praise still arise who help to make the services of God memorable by the melody and spiritual quality of their voice. But one fears the glorious art is passing away, since it cannot survive apart from the sweet pastoral tongue with which the Evangelical movement in the Highlands was so intimately associated.

The Sower who also Reaped.

THE Rev. Duncan MacBeath, who laboured in the district of Ness for thirteen years, came from the Ross-shire mainland. He was a native of Applecross. Both his grandfather and father were sincere followers of the Lord. There was an occasion when the three of them, each representing a generation, spoke at the same Question meeting on a Friday. Duncan MacBeath's father was known as 'The Fair Catechist,' and the son inherited much of the physical comeliness of the father. He was also gifted with an impressive voice, a strong personality, and an unstudied, if unconscious, dramatic gesture. Though remote in manner and grave of disposition, he was not without humour. When, for example, he was on his way to his station in Lewis a man accosted him with the usual question as to 'what might the stranger be doing in the island?' 'I am come,' he said, 'to enlist all who will in the King's army.' 'I suppose,' ventured the wayside rustic, 'it is the young men you will be after?' 'Yes, and the young women too,' was the reply—a reply which, no doubt, left the bewildered questioner wondering if the stranger was not obsessed with rather strange fancies. In answer to a similar question from another he told him that he had come 'to plant trees.' Possibly both parties understood later on the hidden meaning of the gracious wayfarer's parable. That he did enlist many in the Lord's army is true; and under his ministry in Ness the myrtle tree and the fir tree grew where the briar and the thorn had cumbered the ground.

Mr. MacBeath was a man who lived much of his life in the habit of prayer. His word was therefore with power. A person who obtained much blessing under his preaching once told the writer that frequently after a Sabbath service the trickle of tears which had dropped from the eyes of his hearers could be seen on the floor opposite numerous pews. Yet, unlike other 'revivals' since, nothing could be seen or heard calculated to distract either preacher or people.

There was a Christian woman in the district—Margaret Thomson, Skigersta—who once said of Mr. MacBeath: 'I never listened to him but I could say as he finished, O what a pity you were not at the beginning!' Although Margaret had listened to nearly all the great preachers of the day, this was something she could not invariably say of any other.

If Mr. MacBeath often showed severity toward some in whose Christian witness he could put no trust he could, on the other hand, be extremely tender toward the lowly and contrite in heart. In those days there were 'hidden ones' in the land. These were men and women who, oppressed with a sense of sin, never ventured to make a public profession of their hope either by word or in the ordinance. Those he resembled to a hidden stream the wholesome waters of which could not be seen or tasted except at the point where it touched the sea. Those were they, in other words, who walked humbly and in quiet before the Lord, but who often on the very fringe of the eternal world made it clear that they knew the grace of God in truth. 'Private Christians,' as they were sometimes called, were perhaps more numerous on the mainland than in the isles. The noted William Fraser, who lived at Tomnahurich near Inverness, had a son who lived a retired Christian life. Mr. Finlay Cook had a great regard for him, and was most desirous of hearing him at family worship. He, therefore, arranged with Mr. Fraser's sister that he should be given a place of concealment in a large cupboard where he could hear without being seen. This admirable arrangement might have worked well enough only for Mr. Fraser's persistent intuition that there was someone hidden in the house. After a second search for this mysterious and invisible third party Mr. Cook was well and truly located in his cupboard. Needless to say, he had to conduct worship himself. But we are speaking of Duncan MacBeath.

Dr. Kennedy, Dingwall, once preached a powerful sermon in Stornoway. The great herald of God gave seven marks peculiar to the true Christian, while seven were also given to describe the mere formalist. Mr. MacBeath listened to the sermon. An exercised Christian woman who also listened to that sermon was much alarmed to find herself, as she believed, answering to all the fourteen marks given! In a state of fear she went over to Ness a few days afterwards to see if Mr. MacBeath could throw any light on her rather alarming discovery of her own heart. Her surprise knew no bounds when Mr. MacBeath, in the course of his sermon, said, 'You are here today who heard Dr. Kennedy giving marks which described the righteous and the hypocrite, and you are afraid because you seem to find all these in your own bosom. If that is your case, my soul for your soul, that you will never enter a lost eternity.'

There was another choice Christian woman in the district whose mind was much exercised over a portion of Scripture. Dissatisfied with her own grasp of its meaning she asked one or two elders of the Church if they could explain it. This they were unable to do. That very day on the way to a service she prayed earnestly that Mr. MacBeath might handle the passage in his sermon. As he stood up to preach he informed the people that he had a message prepared, but that his mind was irresistably drawn to another portion of the Word. There and then he read the words which had so much occupied the woman who sat somewhere in the crowd. In his treatment of the words he enjoyed great freedom. The word was with unusual power. When the service ended he left the Church unwilling to speak to any in the way. Only the person whose prayer God had so richly answered stood before him. She asked him if the sermon which he had just delivered was the fruit of his own experience. ' I cannot say that it was,' he replied, ' but I believe what I said was true in the experience of some. And are you,' he added, ' the woman who took from me the sermon? I wonder how many in Ness could take the sermon from the minister as you have done! '

Duncan MacBeath was no stranger to temptation. Once he asked a trusted friend to pray that a temptation which he knew was on the way might pass him by. ' That I cannot do,' was the answer, ' but I shall pray that the Lord may support you under it, and open a way of escape for your soul.' He admitted that this saying was more scriptural than his own desire that the temptation should not overtake him.

It is the lot of those whose prayers are heard to sorrow over the corruptions and imperfections which mar all their devotions. Duncan MacBeath once remarked that the prayers of God's people, however vile in their own eyes, were in all their purity and fragrance preserved in the golden vials in Heaven. The prayers of the broken in heart were sanctified by Christ the Altar, through whose merits they were offered to God.

One evening after having preached a sermon bathed in power, and which filled his own soul and that of many of his hearers with much consolation, he prayed in these words: ' Thou hast given this great deliverance into the hand of thy servant: and now shall I die for thirst ' (Judges xv. 18). The prayer indicated that the enjoyment of such a blessing only increases the longings of the soul for the fuller realisation of the pleasures which are reserved at God's right hand in heaven.

Like so many of the Highland ministers, Mr. MacBeath had the art of presenting abstract ideas in pictorial language. The permanence, even in Heaven, of the three superlative graces of faith, hope and love he once mentioned in a sermon. ' We know that love never fails; but where do faith and hope go when the redeemed enter heaven? Ah, friend, when you stand on the threshold of glory your faith shall be swallowed up in sight and your hope in possession.'

Thomas Boston had also many choice things to say on this attractive theme.

In ministering comfort to those who were 'chosen in the furnace of affliction,' he could use words of love and tenderness. 'The Heavenly Refiner has His eye, not on the finished and purified gold which lies up on His shelves, but on that which is in the furnace lest it should be left there a moment longer than is necessary.' The suffering saints on earth, in other words, enjoy God's special care in a way unneeded by those who stand faultless before the Throne.

When he mentioned the free offer of the Gospel to perishing men he pointed often to the door of heaven which Christ left open when He passed into the Holiest with His own blood. He would assure his unconverted hearers of the welcome awaiting all who would strive to enter into life. 'Methinks,' he said once, 'when Christ entered heaven he commanded the angels saying: "See that the gates are always open."'

There is in Lewis a little hill which goes by the lovely name of 'The Hill of Two Views' (Cnoc an da sheallaidh). From the top of this Hebridean Mizar on a clear day one may, on looking eastward, see the waters of the Minch, while westward lies the blue expanse of the Atlantic. Making use of this natural fact Mr. MacBeath once said that at the place where the convicted sinner has the clearest sight of his sin, there also God showed him the sea of the infinite merits of Christ's blood where his sin can be covered for ever.

A young Lewisman once travelling home had to lodge a night in Stromeferry. In the house where he stayed there was an elderly lady who enquired for Mr. Duncan MacBeath. She was anxious that he would convey a message to the people among whom he laboured. Her message was that they should not oppose him in his work as the Lord was with him. In his hearing she related instances of some in her own country who had come under God's displeasure for trying to hurt him in his labours for Christ. If some otherwise worthy men in Lewis had heard of this exhortation they might have hesitated before allowing a tragic rift to take place in their friendship with their minister.

During the last years of his ministry he was accustomed to speak of the 'dark clouds' which he saw gathering over the nations and over the visible Church. The Free Church of that time was in a state of upheaval through the introduction of the so-called modernistic view put forward by men like Professor Robertson Smith. The issue at stake was the trustworthiness of the Bible as God's inerrant Word. 'When Satan wants to play havoc in the Church of God he picks the smartest horse in the stable' was Duncan MacBeath's way of expressing how these intellectually able men were Satan's tools to infect the Church with a plague the end of which none could predict.

A few weeks before he passed away Mr. MacBeath was at a communion in Knockbain. On the way home he preached a most impressive sermon in Barvas on the words of the Bride in the Songs: 'Until the day break and the shadows flee away I will get me to the mountain of myrrh and to the hill of frankincense.' The sermon had a melting effect on the hearts of the Lord's people. It seemed to them as if the messenger and the voice were on the fringe of the world of glory. Some of them wept afterwards outside because they felt they would hear him no more. He had, perhaps unconsciously, preached his farewell message to many present.

The crop of converts which came into existence under Mr. MacBeath's preaching was noted for the stable quality of their spiritual life. They grew and matured in the devotional atmosphere of a congregation on which a copious shower of the divine blessing had fallen. If in after years some of them lost the sensible enjoyment of their first love there were few, indeed, who fell away. In his old age one of them told a friend of the spiritual joy of his early days, but how a gradual decay left him nothing but a mournful recollection of better times. This state of felt spiritual decline lasted for twenty years. ' But one day,' he related, ' as I sat listening to the Word preached, I felt what I was afraid had utterly died within me springing again to life.' The Lord opened his grave and gave him a longed-for reviving. When the mown grass gets ' the latter rain ' a new growth is at hand.

In his last illness the words ' loose him and let him go ' came to his mind with much power. He took these words to mean that the Lord would again release him from the bonds of affliction and give him fresh strength to proclaim His Word. When he mentioned his hope concerning these words to one of his friends the remark was made: ' The news is good for you, Mr. MacBeath, but not for us.' He then saw that the words carried a message from the King that the time to cross the river had come.

The Sabbath before he died he left the manse with his text chosen and the sermon thought out. When, however, he stood up to preach he confessed to the people that by an inward compulsion he had to change his theme. He gave out the words: ' Awake, O sword against my shepherd, and against the man that is my fellow, saith the Lord of hosts; smite the shepherd, and the sheep shall be scattered . . . ' These words, we know, refer to the eternal Son of God Who had to bear the stroke of divine justice because He bore our sins. It was, however, both significant and solemn that within a few days the dust of this faithful pastor of Christ was carried to the grave amid the tears which dropped from thousands of eyes. He died in 1891 at the age of seventy years.

His venerable cousin, Mr. Finlay MacRae, of Knockbain and Plockton, preached his funeral sermon from the words, ' And Enoch walked with God; and he was not, for God took him.' His dust lies among a people who, when the effort was made to compel his departure, would not part with him, and from whose midst he was the means of bringing many to the Lord. The words inscribed on his stone of memorial are therefore an appropriate commentary on his ministry: ' And they that be wise shall shine as the brightness of the firmament; and they that turn many to righteousness as the stars for ever and ever.'

The words of Rachel MacLeod of Bragar express in touching words the loss felt by all when this righteous man was taken away from the earth. I give three verses in the original Gaelic:

> 'Se muintir Nis a fhuair an leagadh,
> Maighstir MacBeth air a thoirt uath';
> 'S iomadh suil tha 'n diugh ri sileadh,
> 'S fear togail an cridhe anns an uaigh.
>
> Ged bhiodh an t-uaireadar bu bhoicheadh
> Na do phoca 's ri do chluais,
> Cha 'n eisdidh tu ris a cheol aic',
> 'S tu 'g innseadh mu ghloir an Uain.
>
> An uair ainneamh chluinninn fhein thu,
> Chuireadh tu faoilte orm le buaidh,
> Dh' fhagadh tu lathaireachd aig m'anam,
> Nach dealaich rium fad mo chuairt.*

Since then the island of Lewis has had its periodical revivals right down through the years. There were ministers whom God took to Himself in the midst of their usefulness, and whose labours were owned.

In the early years of this century a local but genuine revival began in the district of Carloway under the excellent Mr. George MacKay, then minister at Stornoway, and latterly at Fearn. A preliminary to this time of refreshing was an effort on the part of Mr. MacKay to break up a big party which had gathered in a large barn to celebrate a village marriage. Mr. MacKay had conducted the marriage ceremony the evening before, and there he formed the opinion that a night of unbecoming revelry was contemplated. Driven out of bed by a conscience which kept sleep at bay he arrived at the scene of celebration about two in the morning. After several escapades, which assumed the character of a complicated military strategy, he succeeded in capturing the entire barn and two melodeons! A lame and angry piper held out to the last, but he succeeded in breaking up what proved to be an unseemly gathering.

The following day Mr. MacKay conducted a service at which he preached from the words, ' Have no fellowship with the unfruitful works of darkness, but rather reprove them.' God owned his faithfulness, for some in the audience lived to bless God for a sermon which was the means of awakening them to righteousness.

Donald MacLeod, the catechist, was one of the men on whom the spiritual care of the district devolved after the death of Mr. MacBeath. A man of holy zeal, he redeemed time and opportunity in the service of his Lord. I shall give one instance of his Christian earnestness, and its rather strange sequel. He was present one night in a home in Habost, Ness, which death had visited. After the usual act of worship a man present made a commonplace remark about the weather, and how some shrewd men could tell beforehand what the weather might be like during the coming days. This gave Donald MacLeod an opportunity to introduce a higher and more profitable theme. He enlarged on how holy men of God from the very beginning of time foretold the coming of that Just One who was to redeem men. The deep impression he made on the company was unmistakable. He felt a breach had been made on the kingdom of darkness. But Satan, or one of his emissaries, had his revenge. A fearless man, without a trace of superstition in his nature, he was that night on his way home greatly buffeted by a tall, sinister stranger who threatened him with dire punishment for his words in the house he had just left.   Donald could never explain this incident, but it led him to put himself more and more under God's protecting care.

Donald Gunn, a younger contemporary of Donald MacLeod, was a man of great simplicity of heart. In his youth he emigrated to South Africa, and while there God brought him under a harrowing conviction of his sin.   In the dark shadows of spiritual distress he concluded that he was outwith the number whom God loved in Christ from all eternity.   One day, walking in a solitary way, he sat down beneath a rock.   There, and out of the loneliness and fear of that hour, he heard a song.   As he listened he saw coming toward him, arm in arm, a band of coloured girls singing the words—

" Jesus loves me this I know
For the Bible tells me so."

These words God used to liberate his imprisoned spirit, and to introduce into his soul the first sweet taste of His wonderful grace.

Donald never ceased to speak of his affection for those little children, the unconscious messengers of good tidings to his soul.

*"English translation of Gaelic poem on page 70".

What a loss the people of Ness have sustained.
In being deprived of Mr MacBeath
Many eyes are today shedding tears,
Since their comforter is in the grave.

Though the most elegant time-piece
Were in your pocket or at your ear,
You would not heed its chiming
As you declared the glory of the Lamb.

On the rare occasion that I heard you
You effectively cheered my spirits,
And you left with my soul a presence
Which will not depart from me during life's journey.

'The Doctor.'

IF Dr. John MacDonald, by his incessant labours, gave breadth to the evangelical movement in the Highlands, Dr. Kennedy gave it solidity and depth. These two men were the Luther and the Calvin of the north.

Though these two were supreme in their generation for pulpit eloquence and for a rich variety of great gifts there was a minister in Ross-shire who, for depth of piety and personal holiness, excelled them both. I refer to Charles Calder of Ferintosh.

This holy herald of God was a man of calm assurance and Christlike bearing. His lucid and wonderful sermons invariably dwelt on two themes—the love of Christ, and the infinite wisdom displayed in God's way of salvation. But for all his love-bathed qualities he was no stranger to the terrors of temptations. Sometimes a spirit of atheism would assail his mind. One night as he gazed on a lovely sky replete with evidences of God's glory he remarked: 'Who would now say that there is no God?'

He was not the first to feel the liberating effect which comes through contemplating a universe which declares the glory of the Lord.

With all his spiritual calmness Mr. Calder knew how to warn the sinner. During a service once some of the people on the fringe of the congregation began to move away before he had finished. He sternly rebuked them by saying: 'A wind from hell is rising, and the chaff is being driven away.'

The last sermon which he preached at Ferintosh was a remarkable utterance. As he finished his sermon that day he

looked round the congregation and said: 'I have an impression
either that I am speaking today, or some of you are hearing,
for the last time; and before we part for ever I shall call five
great witnesses to avouch that I have declared to you the whole
counsel of God. The first is God the Father, the omniscient
and heart-searching God. I call Him to witness that I have
set before you life and death. The second is God the
Son. I call Him to witness that He has been the burden
of my preaching during those thirty-eight years. The third is
God the Holy Spirit. I call Him to witness that I have set
before you the nature, marks and fruits of His work, and the
necessity of the new birth. The fourth great witness is the
Bible. And the fifth is the company of elect angels who are
now waiting to rejoice over your conversion. With these I call
your own consciences. I call also the stones and timbers of this
house to witness that I have not shunned to declare the whole
counsel of God.'

With these words Charles Calder closed the Bible and came
down the pulpit stairs for the last time.

Doctor MacDonald was, however, the most outstanding
evangelical preacher in his generation in the north. Yet there
were those, even in his own congregation, who would occasionally
wander from his fold to feed on other pastures. And thereby
hangs a tale.

His session, on one occasion, brought in a complaint against
a certain woman who was in the habit of worshipping sometimes
in the neighbouring parishes of Killearnan and Resolis. The
good woman freely admitted her fault. When asked by the
genial doctor the reason for her conduct she replied that in
Killearnan the sheep were fed, while at Resolis the lambs were
provided with the sincere milk of the Word. 'And what happens
here,' hesitatingly asked her minister. The impressive answer
was—'Here the dead are raised.' It was a great compliment
to a man whom God owned more perhaps in the conversion of

sinners than in the nourishing and comforting of God's people in their needs and trials.

But this chapter we devote to a younger friend of Dr. MacDonald—the famous John Kennedy of Dingwall.

Dr. Kennedy was not a narrow sectarian. He was ever the affectionate companion of all who loved the Truth whatever their distinctive ecclesiastical persuasion. In America he felt very much at home in the famous Princeton College. When he built his new Church in Dingwall the incomparable Baptist, Mr. C. H. Spurgeon, travelled north to preach at the opening services. The Church utterly failed to accommodate the immense crowds which gathered to hear the famous preacher. Mr. Spurgeon preached for an hour from the words, 'The other disciple said unto him, we have seen the Lord' (John xx. 25). It was a characteristic sermon. He revelled in his theme like a strong eagle soaring into his limitless element. In the evening of that day he spoke again to an audience of about six thousand from the words, 'Wisdom is justified in her children.' There was a lovely touch about this service. On his way to the service he picked a blue-eyed 'forget-me-not' which he placed conspicuously in his buttonhole. Many in the crowd who wondered what this floral adornment could mean were delighted when at the end of the sermon he said, 'I stuck this little flower in my buttonhole; it is a "forget-me-not," and to you who have heard I would say—Forget-me-not, and if you forget me, do not forget what I have said.'

Dr. Kennedy himself, though lacking in some of Mr. Spurgeon's qualities, had few equals as a preacher. His intensely theological sermons he clothed in literary garments which showed how deep was his knowledge of that 'well of English undefiled' —the Authorised Version of the Bible. He knew all the Puritans. He could also illustrate his sermons with great felicity. One could give many examples of this, but the following should suffice to show his way of letting the light stream through his

message. Once at a communion in Creich he dwelt on the
words, ' As far as the east is from the west, so far hath He
removed our transgressions from us.' After referring to the
vast distance between east and west, and the great oceans which
roll between, he spoke of ' the seas ' which separate for ever
the believer from the guilt and condemnation of his sins. There
is the infinite sea of the electing and everlasting love of the
Father; there is the sea of the infinite merits of the Eternal
Son in His atoning death; and there is the sea of the love of
God shed abroad in our hearts by the Holy Spirit which He
has given us.

The love of the Triune God to the Church was a favourite
theme. To him it was a fathomless deep, out of which we
could only ' taste ' in this life. He once said, ' When I stand
on the shore, I can see with my eyes but a small part of the
far stretching sea. There is a limit to what mine eye can
perceive. My mind, however, can comprehend more than the
eye can see. Yet of this plenitude I can only lift a few drops
to my lips in the hollow of my hand.' He may run who reads
the meaning of these words.

On another occasion he said: ' The love of Christ for the
Church is infinitely rich and infinitely holy. But be not afraid
that the holiness of His love will ever come between its riches
and your soul. Though your soul is full of sin the holiness of
that love will have its revenge on that which made it vile . . .
Many, indeed, are the spots upon you, but if you come to Christ
with them all you will never regret it. I heard the Lord com-
plaining of those who did not come to Him with their sins,
but never of those who came . . . All is given you through
the blood, and there is not in your own sinful heart on earth
or in hell beneath that can keep you from Christ. The end
of His love is that He might present the Church to Himself
" without spot." There shall not be found on them on that
Day the least mark of the devil's teeth or of hell's malice. The

name of the Lamb shall be on their forehead, but through all Eternity the scars of their trials and temptations shall never be seen.'

In those days men and women thought twice before coming to the Lord's Table. The wholesome fear of partaking 'unworthily' often caused serious reflections and long hesitations. This was true even of choice believers. For the encouragement of such he once used the following illustration on a communion Sabbath: 'I seem to see an abundant feast spread before the Lord's poor ones. They fear, however, that the good things are not for them. They look longingly at the table, but who is worthy to sit down thereat? But I seem to see a young man in the company who ventures nearer to the table than the rest. He would know what are those letters of gold inscribed on a covering which hides the contents of a dish on the table. And this is what he reads, "A gift of choice honey from the Elder Brother to the children to be divided among themselves." With that they all come, and receive that which by His death He provides.'

On another occasion he said with regard to the state of God's people as they were found by Christ 'dead in sin:' 'When Christ came to marry his Bride it was far more likely He would have to bury her—death seemed much more imminent than life. And I tell you how the matter stood with myself. I died; and the day of my death was the day of my resurrection, birth and marriage. This was also the way John Bunyan felt, aye, and many other Johns besides.'

One of the 'Men' in giving his testimony on a Friday remarked that the word of pardon came to him 'written in blood.' Dr. Kennedy afterwards took up his parable and said: 'If you obtained your pardon written in blood it was given you to see that only through the blood of the Great Sacrifice could your pardon be sealed and your soul redeemed. If you obtained your pardon written in blood much as you valued the pardon and the salvation it brought you, you valued the blood through which the pardon came more than the pardon itself. And if you obtained your pardon written in blood much as you valued the pardon and the blood through which the pardon reached you, you value more than all the Person whose blood sealed your pardon and who in love forgave you your sin.' This remark in the original Gaelic has a literary rhythm and grace which are quite absent in any translation.

One of his most remarkable sermons was on God building up Zion. Beginning with a description of how God laid her foundations from all eternity in the Council of Peace, he went on to trace her growth and development, her ' Corner Stone ' and her ' living stones,' till he came to ' the topstone thereof.' As he viewed the glorious edifice complete and raised up to God he paused, looked up, and said: ' It has passed out of my view into eternal glory. I can see it no more.' This sermon, delivered in characteristic style by walking to and fro on his spacious platform, and holding the ever present white handkerchief in his hand, made a lasting impression on many.

Dr. Kennedy, like his Lord and His prophets and apostles, was not a believer in the so-called ' positive ' preaching by which the Truth only is supposed to be proclaimed but error never exposed nor condemned.

In contrast to his sermon on God's chosen Zion this is how, for example, the faithful herald of the north speaks of the Roman Church: ' O thou mother of harlots there is more effectual prayer against thee in the shrieks of the millions thou hast delivered over to the great murderer who retains thee for the work of slaying souls, than there is to shield thee from destruction in all the devotions of which thy polluted altars and thy dark cloisters are the scenes. The millions thou hast ruined curse thee from the pit. The thousands thou hast martyred cry by their blood for thy destruction. They shall be heard, and thou shalt yet be laid low.'

This condemnation of an anti-christian system is a long way from the foolish hope of many in these perilous times that the Roman Church is a bulwark against the evils of the age. To John Kennedy Romanism itself was the greatest evil that has ever darkened this planet.

It was but rarely that Dr. Kennedy preached under the mantle of a prophet. When he delivered himself of some pronouncement related to the Church of God, either in the far or near future, his words were well weighed. They were invariably the outcome of light obtained by means of prayer and the written Word. In one remarkable sermon on Isaiah xxvi. verse 20, he predicted the decline of evangelical preaching in the land. The beginnings of this falling away he had observed in his own day. The Lord, he remarked, would remove His loving witnesses, and few would arise to fill their place. False but popular teaching would displace the Gospel of free grace, and a generation without spiritual discernment would drink the poison like as a blind man would drink unwholesome water out of an unclean vessel. A spirit of worldliness would overcome the people, and the means of grace would be largely forsaken. God's Spirit would be grieved and therefore denied. In such a day the Lord's people would be few, feeble and hidden. This was a prediction which stood out in sharp contrast to the shallow optimism of those who in his day spoke of science, religion, and an ascending humanity, walking hand in hand to inaugurate an era of peace, moral progress, and spiritual life. But Time and God's Providence have fulfilled Dr. Kennedy's sombre vision—even in its very details.

On a communion Sabbath in Stornoway he expressed his fear that one present at the ordinance would that day be suddenly summoned into God's Presence. Later on in the day Dr. Kennedy spoke quietly to Mr. Hector Cameron, Back, about the burden resting on his mind since giving expression to his presentiment. Almost immediately they were told that a good woman who was present at the service died on the way home.

This was how Dr. Kennedy expounds that lovely phrase—' the bundle of life.' The words are found in Abigail's beautifully persuasive speech before King David. ' The bundle of life is that which contains the people of God—the electing love of the Father, the Eternal Council and the everlasting covenant being the folds of the wrapping; the Son's love, merit and power preserving them till called; then the Spirit's grace bringing them out of the bundle of death, with its four folds of death in sin, death from the power of Satan, death from the curse of a broken law, death through the influence of the world. By His uniting them to Christ they are put into the bundle of life—folded in the love of God, covered with the righteousness of Christ, and hid with Him in God.'

The multitudes of exercised Christian people to whom Dr. Kennedy ministered in the Highlands of those days demanded wide sympathy and spiritual understanding. He once comforted those whose spiritual consolations were small by saying that at some marriages a very rich feast might be provided, while poorer folk might have but little. But the marriage tie was as secure in the one case as in the other. Soul union with Christ, and not our sensible enjoyments, in other words, was what mattered.

' If,' he once said, ' you were wounded in battle you would rather your wound be dressed by one who had been once wounded himself, and who could be touched with a feeling of your pain. There is but One who can so minister to the broken in heart.' Another remark of his goes to show how our state here is related to the dispensations of the all wise God in the covenant of peace. ' If one drop of trouble were to go amissing, so that you did not drink of it, it would bring a reproach on the covenant.'

The clouds which come between the soul and the Sun of Righteousness are part of our broken life here. 'A cloud received Him out of their sight.' Commenting on this phrase, he said that however near our view of Christ in this world of time the vision would surely fade. Only beyond time shall the perfect day dawn, and the day star arise in our hearts.

He once spoke of the poor in spirit and those who have no help of man. A man may be poor, but as long as he is able to earn his living, and there is a living to earn, we would not deem him poor. A man may be poor, and through infirmity unable to earn his daily bread, but if there are those who are able to help him we should not consider him wholly poor. The poor man is he who has lost all ability to help himself, and who has no friend on earth to relieve him. It is so with Christ's poor ones. Of themselves they can do nothing. No man cares for their souls. They therefore look to Christ alone for their strength. He alone becomes their portion in the land of the living.

The grace of an unclouded assurance is not an easy attainment. Many choice souls go to Heaven trembling lest when they come to the door they should be unknown to God as His own. On one occasion in Lewis he quoted the following words from Psalm 62:

'In God my glory placed is and my salvation sure.'

'These words,' he remarked, 'would choke some of the Lord's people; but let me go on to read words which suit them all.' He then quoted the following verse with its tender invitation to trust and to pray:

'Ye people place your confidence
in him continually:
Before him pour ye out your heart:
God is our refuge high.'

He was once asked by a Christian lady how it was that, unlike his father, he so seldom prayed in public for the promised day of millennium glory. He replied that he had been given such a terrifying view of those tribulations which must necessarily precede that longed-for age that the courage to plead its promise in public had almost left him.

Others have felt this too.

Not only in the pulpit was John Kennedy a faithful witness. In his dealings with individuals he never failed in setting before them the path of safety. To young people coming under the responsibilities of wedlock, or under baptismal vows, he would say: ' Let God be worshipped in your home; for the home which is without a family altar is like a house without a roof—exposed to every storm, and unsheltered from every danger.'

A remarkable instance of his spiritual sensitivity occurred one night as he was travelling in his coach towards Conon Bridge. In the darkness they overtook a solitary wayfarer to whom Dr. Kennedy said: ' Come in here; for whoever you are I felt your prayers warming the way before me.' The good man was Simon Campbell of Kilmorack.

At the Friday fellowship meeting Dr. Kennedy was in the habit of grouping together speakers whose Christian names were identical. ' Donalds ' and ' Johns,' and so on, were thus listed together till all had spoken. Farquhar MacLennan, Strathconon, and afterwards an elder at Contin, once attended a fellowship meeting in Dingwall over which Dr. Kennedy presided. Farquhar was no stranger to temptation. Before leaving for Dingwall on this occasion the worthy man was tempted to believe that no one bearing his name was ever a subject of saving grace! Under the power of this apparently silly, but to him very sore, temptation he sat anxiously in the Church. It so happened that on this particular day the doctor had listed together a goodly cluster of ' Farquhars.' Hearing three of them speak in succession, Farquhar MacLennan could no longer contain his joy and sense of relief. As if addressing an invisible enemy he cried out, ' You were a liar from the beginning; there are three here who bear the name of Farquhar, and now I hope I also may be among the Farquhars redeemed by the blood of Christ.' That communion was a green spot in the tried life of this man of God.

Such interruptions would in no way disconcert the preacher or hearer. A simple-minded woman, once listening to Dr. Kennedy, found his sermon greatly beyond her reach. ' You are too high, doctor; come down here where we are,' she exclaimed. Immediately, and with great tenderness, he set about to adapt his message to her level.

As Dr. Kennedy grew in grace his sense of sin deepened. In his own eyes he was 'the chief of sinners' to the end. He once said in addressing communicants at the famous green hollow outside Gairloch (known as ' the white cow's bed '): ' If my brethren knew all that passed through my mind since I left the manse today they would cold-shoulder me for ever.' A good man who heard this remark was displeased that the doctor should, in so great and so mixed a company, uncover the plague of his own heart. But the same man lived to thank God that those words fell from the lips of one of whom he was sure that he knew the Lord and His grace.

Like his father before him Dr. Kennedy was a man of fine Christian sympathy. If the phrase ' the communion of saints ' ever wanted an illustration of its meaning we could find it in the life of the Kennedys.

When the worthy David Steven, Caithness, was taken away to his rest, Dr. Kennedy wrote: ' I cannot tell you how I feel it when I miss him out of my prayers, and when in thinking over the cause of Christ I have him no longer to put into the scale in which I usually place the tokens of good when weighing them against the signs of judgment. Many a sweet moment have I spent in spirit in David's cottage . . . Now death has

been there and his place is empty . . . But Christ has another
mansion filled . . . another jewel in His crown.' Who can
measure the value of such fellowship. ' Behold how good and
how pleasant it is for brethren to dwell together in unity.' (Psalm
cxxxiii. 1).

Such a bond of spiritual union in the Lord was a precious
characteristic of the older evangelical believers. We saw how
it existed in the case of Catherine and John MacKay. William
Fraser, Inverness, and John Kennedy, Killearnan, kept family
worship in the evening at the same hour. Any interruption of
this arrangement they instantly became aware of.

James Calder of Croy has in interesting entry in his diary
bearing on this subject. ' When,' he writes, ' I began family
worship this forenoon, with singing at the beginning of Psalm
ciii., I was much impressed that my dear and heavenly brother,
Mr. MacPhail (Resolis) had begun his everlasting song with
Christ in Paradise. The impression became stronger in time of
prayer, and upon retiring after worship I could not help breaking
into a flood of tears for my sweetest, dearest, and most precious
friend; not for himself, but for the Church of Christ.' Two days
afterwards the excellent Mr. Calder writes again: ' Received
the mournful news of what was so strongly impressed on my
mind on Sabbath morning: the death of the most eminently
pious . . . minister of Christ I ever saw . . . and the most
lovely image of his adorable Lord that ever I knew. He was
exceedingly high in the sphere of grace below, and many shall
be his jewels to adorn his crown.'

In the letter of sympathy which Mr. Spurgeon wrote after
the death of Dr. Kennedy he mentions his seasons of spiritual
conflict. Mr. Spurgeon himself, as he hints in his letter, and as
so many of his sermons reveal, was no stranger to frequent
overshadowings of spirit. Dr. Kennedy, like his intimate friend,
Dr. C. C. MacIntosh, of Tain and Dunoon, knew the misery of
walking in darkness, without light. Perhaps what he wrote of

the famed Mr. Porteous of Kilmuir was true also of his own life: 'He could be no stranger to Satan's devices; for having so many of the Lord's children to feed it was needful, as their pastor, that he should pass through their trials besides as a Christian experiencing his own.' Although he could conceal his inward state from the public before whom he ministered his friends at times could not fail to get a glimpse of the depths of anguish from which he so often cried to God. He once broke down in the presence of his Session saying: 'Who knows but I may yet be saved?' These hidden sorrows gave his mind a tenderness toward the afflicted soul who needed encouragement in the way. One of his hearers used to tell her friends how as she sat one day listening to him she mourned over her spiritual emptiness and her lack of a clear view of her interest in Christ. Just then the melodious voice rang forth: 'It matters not whether your interest in Christ is clear to you; if you can truly say that you feel your need of Him.' Thus he could travel with his flock in all their spiritual anxieties.

The typical Highland Christian of Dr. Kennedy's age has sometimes been misrepresented as introspective and seldom, if ever, able to reach that place in the spiritual life where the soul rejoices in the assurance of God's love. The fact is, however, that in the Highlands, as elsewhere, all degrees and complexions of the Christian life could be found. One of the ' Men ' once remarked that he had never seen two faces exactly alike, and he had never met with any two of the Lord's people whose experiences, at all points, coincided. There is a sweet variety in all the works of God—both in nature and in grace.

John Bunyan, in his Heaven-sent Dream, presents us with a glorious company of pilgrims. They had many things in common. They all came in at the gate; they all had stood by the Cross, and they all rejoiced in the hope of seeing Christ's face in righteousness in Mount Zion. But how refreshingly different they all were both in their dispositions and in the content of their experiences as seekers after God. In the North, as elsewhere, one could meet with Mercy in her white garments of assurance, and also with Mr. Fearing, trembling lest he should be refused entrance at the gate.

A young minister once called on a blind Christian lady in the North. She deprecated the habit of those who seemed to glory in their doubts and denials. ' As for myself, dear,' she said, ' I never tried to conceal from the Lord or His people the worth of mine inheritance.'

On the other hand many would sympathise with the much tried saint who, at a fellowship meeting, expressed his faith in trembling words: " For over sixty years I am professing to be on the Rock which is Christ; but my fear today is that my hope is not resting on that sure Foundation.' But this was too much for the presiding minister who knew the worth of his man. He stood up in the pulpit, and in a voice of thunder cried out: ' You are on it, William! You are on it! You are on it! '

When Dr. Kennedy passed within the veil a lifelong friend in Caithness in whose home he was always a welcome guest, saw him one night in a dream. As she went forward to welcome him he said: ' Touch me not, for you are so cold down in this world.' Remembering that he had passed away she ventured the question: ' What is it that surprised you most since leaving us? ' He replied that it was the discovery that those efforts in the vineyard, which he had thought the Lord had owned bore no lasting fruit, while He blessed that which he considered to be of little worth. It was a remark which should both humble and encourage every servant of God.

The decline which the Church in the North underwent through the impact of other influences was felt by many who lived after Dr. Kennedy's generation had left the scene.

This change was expressed in vivid words by the excellent Peter Fraser of Dornoch. In his old age Peter used to wonder at the ease with which some of his younger friends arrived at a place of safety and rest. They seemed to come out of their Egypt without any knowledge of a pursuing host, a drowning depth, or of the hovering angel of God's Justice. As Peter mused on these things he suddenly remembered that he had lived to see the Flying Age, when men could with apparent ease surmount all such difficulties. It was the age when the doctrine of sin was given a minor emphasis.

A Swift Witness: Alexander MacColl.

THERE was another minister in the north who, whatever the reason, is not so well known as either Dr. MacDonald or Dr. Kennedy. I refer to Mr. Alexander MacColl, who died at Lochalsh in 1889. Without comparing him to these two in point of personal influence and gifts, he was, in the opinion of many, a spiritual star of the first magnitude.

As a child he was baptised by the renowned Mr. Lachlan MacKenzie of Lochcarron. After the ordinance had been dispensed the minister tenderly commended him to his parents' care, remarking that he had seen a ray of light from Heaven falling on his soul, and that he would live to preach the Gospel.

On a subsequent occasion Mr. MacKenzie predicted that his ministry would be blessed especially in the conversion of many whose heads were grey with age. It is remarkable that not only was his ministry singularly blessed in the conversion of such, but also that his most impressive pulpit appeals were addressed to aged men and women who were still out of Christ.

Mr. MacColl had a sharp awakening and with it came the inevitable 'hour of temptation.' His trial was a familiar one. Was he or was he not one of God's elect people? And he took his own way to determine the answer to that solemn question.

Being present at a place where a meeting was to be held, over which the godly William Urquhart of Assynt presided, he decided that he would not enter the meeting house for so many minutes after the time to begin had passed. If the meeting had begun before he entered he would take that as a sure sign

his name was not in the Book of Life! This was a precarious
as well as a presumptuous test. When he entered alone, William
Urquhart, who had not commenced the service, turned to him
and said, ' Alexander, do not again limit the Holy One of Israel.'

In passing let me relate one incident in the life of William
Urquhart as told by himself. This eminent Christian was, along
with a friend, on one occasion on the way to Gospel ordinances.
While they sat down to break bread by a moorland pathway
William began to tell his friend of God's dealings with him
when he was a young man in Assynt. He told, among other
things, of how one day as he prayed in a solitary place he saw
a young man sitting on a stone, and playing on a harp. Deeply
affected by the unearthly quality of the music he went forward
and asked what tune he played. ' That,' said the young man,
' was the song which the angels of God are now singing as they
carry home the soul of Robert MacLeod.' It so happened that
the excellent Robert had died exactly at that hour. But this
by the way.

Thomas Goodwin was Alexander MacColl's favourite Puritan
writer. From this deep theological fountain he received inspir-
ation and light. Those transcendant themes with which Goodwin
deals Mr. MacColl ever kept to the forefront of his message.
But he was indebted to no man for his knowledge of Christ.
There were those who looked upon Alexander MacColl as one
who had ' the secret of the Lord.' He often warned his people
of ' things to come.' On one such occasion he remarked that
because of Sabbath desecration God's judgment would one day
reduce the great industrial Clydeside so low that only a few
smokes could be seen from its innumerable chimneys. Clydeside
has had already its death-dealing visitations, but not yet to the
awful scale predicted by this man of God.

When Mr. MacColl was minister at Fort Augustus plans
were under way to erect the Benedictine monastery there. Some
knew that he often prayed that those who engaged in erecting

that desolating building might not succeed. It is a curious fact
that as long as he lived the work was either retarded or at a
standstill.

In Skye he was surrounded by an excellent band of men.
The most lively personality who moved in his orbit there was
Hector MacLean of Hamara. Hector was in Church one day
and noticed some in the audience to whom Gaelic was an
unknown tongue. The sermon was impressive to those who
could understand it. As Mr. MacColl was drawing toward the
end of his discourse Hector exclaimed—' Alexander, if you have
a shot to spare in English will you let these strangers have it! '

Mr. MacColl was a much tried man. There was, indeed, a
season when his mental afflictions accumulated with crushing
severity, and during which he left his parish for some foreign
clime where he might enjoy rest from trouble. It was on a
railway station in Glasgow that the Lord by His Word arrested
his footsteps. He returned home. Perhaps he suffered most at
the hands of those who should have defended him from the evil
tongue. But his private and public trials the Lord richly blessed
to his soul. Once he asked a congregation the question, ' And
what kind of man would you like as your minister? For myself
I would like that minister who had been scorched by the Law,
melted by the Gospel, and much sifted by the temptations of
Satan.'

He was also a man of excellent presence and of an impressive
delivery in the pulpit. He was gifted with a golden voice. In
Glenmoriston, where he laboured for seven years, he once
preached a remarkable sermon from the words—' He that is
surety for a stranger shall smart for it.' This sermon was
long remembered as a powerful and melting exposition on the
sufferings of Him Who became surety for sinners who were
strangers to God.

As this popular minister moved from place to place he had
a tail of admirers. One of these, Miss Kate Gordon, settled

down in Fort Augustus during his ministry there. Kate knew
her minister. One evening, after he had sharply rebuked a
girl who carried on her head a hat of many feathers, she said
to him after the service, 'You should allure them to the Lord
first before you begin to attack their hats.'

He had many things to say of those who provided themselves with excuses for their persistent absence from God's house.
'I have but little hope for dry shod godliness,' he would remark
concerning those who stayed at home because of a shower of
rain. 'There is hope for the formalist, but none for the slothful'
was another of his sayings. The formalist would be seen where
the Gospel was preached, but the slothful man would drowse
in his home.

In all the places where he laboured, in Lochcarron, Duirinish,
Fort Augustus and Lochalsh, his preaching, prayers and personality left an impression which even now survives. There was
a gracious lady in Lochalsh who, in speaking of his holy life,
said, 'Mr. MacColl's prayers on behalf of this place shall continue to be answered to the end of time.'

Alexander MacColl was a swift witness against all appearance
of evil. The zeal with which he opposed every form of iniquity
in the community could be truly terrifying. An old man from
Lochalsh once remarked how some complained of severe words
from the pulpit; 'but Mr. MacColl would say more on that
line in one sermon than we now hear in a year.' And the
remarkable thing was that all those faithful messengers of God
were not only revered in their congregations but greatly loved
as well.

Out in North Uist the faithful Mr. John MacRae laboured
for several years. Mr. MacRae's ministry in the isles was not
all plain sailing. When he told Mr. MacColl of 'his distresses
for Christ's sake,' the latter said, 'What you suffer is a mere
pinprick compared to what you must endure as my successor

in Skye.' And so it was. It was in Duirinish that Mr. MacRae, like Mr. MacColl before him, had to pass through his severest public trials.

Alexander MacColl died of a malignant sore which latterly affected his speech. He, however, continued to preach to the end. A person who benefited greatly through his ministry said, ' How mysterious it is that those lips from which the Gospel fell so sweetly should now perish before our eyes! '

It was said that Mr. MacColl once rebuked a man for working on his croft during the hour of public worship. The man, in hard language, resented the word of exhortation. As he laboured among the sheaves Mr. MacColl's only reply was: ' You shall not eat of it.' That evening, according to the custom of the time, the man gave his wife some of the grain to have it dried, bruised and sifted for their evening meal. But before the meal was ready he had passed away.

At the death bed of another man he cried out in anguish as he tried to pray. The power of evil was so near, so real and so terrible, that he fled in horror from the place.

John MacRae, whom we mentioned, and who succeeded Mr. MacColl at Duirinish, in Skye, was a man of great piety. He was, however, outdistanced by his brother Duncan, who was remarkable in his generation for his prayerfulness and nearness to the Lord. A native of Letterfern, he was known locally by the name of ' Black Duncan.' Mr. MacColl he regarded as one in a thousand. Duncan MacRae once took the ferry across Lochbroom in the company of Mr. George MacLeod, the Free Church minister of that parish. They were unknown to each other. Mr. MacLeod asked Duncan his name. ' They call me Black Duncan,' was the answer. ' Poor man,' said the other; ' if only you knew how black you are! ' ' Little good would that do me,' Duncan replied, ' unless I knew of what would make me white.' Mr. MacLeod then realised that his fellow traveller was not, as he thought, wrapped in spiritual ignorance.

It was in Lochbroom that Duncan enjoyed one of his rare seasons of spiritual consolation. It was not in the public ordinance that he drank out of the river of life, but alone under an old bridge outside the village of Ullapool. There for several nights he wrestled with the Angel 'who blessed him there.' On returning home he went to bed utterly exhausted. He slept continuously for two nights and a day. When he awoke refreshed and well he found an anxious mother sitting by his bedside! C. H. Spurgeon slept through a similar period of time after one of his mighty preaching exertions in London.

When Duncan MacRae visited Lochbroom again he sought the Lord where he had found Him before. But 'the Beloved had withdrawn Himself.' Is God's sovereignty seen more clearly anywhere than in the ebbs and flows of Christian enjoyment?

There was a minister in Glenshiel, not far from Duncan's home, who once gave expression to this alternation of experience in memorable words. His elder spoke one day in his company about the great power and ease with which he preached and how strikingly it contrasted with other times. His minister replied: 'You say that I am empty at times as if the tide had ebbed, and that at other times I am full to overflowing; but does not that prove to you that I am in communion with the Great Deep?'

When Alexander MacColl passed to his rest and reward a pang went to the hearts of those thousands who had come within the sound of his glorious message and his far-reaching and awakening voice.

Valiant for Truth: Donald Duff.

JOHN KENNEDY had his intimate friends among the 'Men.'
There was one, especially, who had an abiding place in his
affections. This was Donald Duff.

Mr. Donald Duff, who laboured in Dingwall for twelve
years as Dr. Kennedy's catechist, was a recognised worthy in
his day. Yet in his own eyes no one was more of a babe in
Christ than he. Born not far from Kingussie, in Inverness-shire,
he was brought up in a home where the Lord was unknown.
For many years the sturdy young pagan went his prayerless way
wholly unconcerned about eternal things. There was, indeed,
one occasion in his youth when confronted with physical danger
he instinctively cried: 'O God help me!' Strangely enough
help came at once, but Donald forgot his Deliverer as soon as the
danger was over.

It was through a sermon preached by Dr. John MacDonald
that he was first awakened to a measure of soul concern. He
was then eighteen years of age. For a season he felt 'a warmth
of the affections,' and becoming outwardly reformed he deceived
both himself and others. Like another he 'received the word
with joy,' but with the first encounter with adversity he sank
into a state of cold compromise. He then sought to make the
best of both worlds.

When harvest time came round Donald, by pipe and dance,
revelled in the annual 'Harvest Home.' On the following
Saturday, however, when he tried to attach himself to a number
of the Lord's people at a meeting of prayer, he was excluded
as one 'whose conduct was not consistent.'

His natural pride recoiled before this rebuff, and for six years he plunged headlong into a life of open defiance to all which belonged to God. He never ceased to marvel at God's forbearance with him during those years of sour rebellion.

It was through the reading of Thomas Boston's *Fourfold State* that an arrow from the King's bow pierced his adamantine heart. For weeks he writhed in mental anguish with this one cry: 'Lord, give me a new heart!' Let him tell the rest of the story in his own words. 'Being in a wood one evening, I bent down and repeated my usual prayer, when all at once I felt as if I was in the presence of God, and that He spoke to me in these words, "What although you should get a new heart! I could not receive you for the sake of your new heart." I was overpowered and self-condemned when in a little these words seemed to follow, "You must be accepted in Another"; and then there was opened up to my view the glorious Person of the Son of God, in power and glory at the Father's right hand! My very soul leaped for amazement and joy, and then and there I received Christ as my Saviour and Lord.'

It was inevitable that after such deliverance and spiritual vision, and after enjoying such a taste of the love which though old is ever new, he should be subjected to many doubts. His powerful mind, with its metaphysical cast, Satan assailed with such questions as the finality of God's sovereignty; the permission of evil; and the freedom of the will. These high questions are not solved by an argument, least of all in an argument with the devil! So like a wise man apprehensive of danger he went to pray.

'I turned,' he said, 'into a field to confess to the Lord my helplessness, and when I was bewailing my case before the All-seeing One it appeared as if all at once the tree of the knowledge of good and evil stood before me, and as if a voice said, "If the tree had stood there until now is there not in your breast what would move you to stretch out your hand to its forbidden fruit? ' This humbled me for I saw that the soul of man freely of its own will took on the guilt of sin. I also got a melting view of the grace that did not destroy the sinner because of disobedience but provided a way of forgiving transgressors to the praise of His mercy and love.'

The next ' fiery dart ' directed at his new-born soul was the suggestion that because he was unweaned from his sin his second attempt to live godly would end more miserably than the first. But no, for he could say then, ' There is in God and only in Him, what will satisfy all my desires.'

From this time he grew in his knowledge of God's Word, of his own heart, and of ' the depths of Satan.' Having lived, for a time, the life of a hypocrite himself, he could never afterwards endure before his eyes any resemblance to that loathsome creature! Where he found his trail or saw his mark he would employ all his weapons to lay him low. Some indeed felt that his censures were severe—especially on those occasions when in speaking on a Friday he would quietly, but often with disconcerting effect, review the experimental quality and doctrinal soundness of the remarks made by other speakers. The Rev. John MacRae, Knockbain, whose sword few' could wield, asked him on one occasion to speak immediately after the Question had been opened. The veteran hesitated, and asked to have the others up first. Mr. MacRae wisely refused. The result was that he spoke with calm power and sweetness, and no personalities were introduced. Outside someone suggested to Mr. MacRae that he should have given Donald Duff time to collect his thoughts. He replied: ' It was good for you I did call him first, and that he did not speak after you. It was a mercy that I also escaped out of his hands.'

When Mr. Spurgeon came to Dingwall in 1870 he was among his numerous hearers. He travelled the following day to Invergordon where his soul was again refreshed by the lips of the incomparable Baptist. The opinion he had formed of

Mr. Spurgeon by reading his sermons did not compare with the impression he made on him by his live and beautiful voice, the impact of his personality, and especially by the felt power accompanying his message. He admired his wonderful gift to present deep doctrine with lucidity and plainness. But what he admired more was his unaffected humility. ' An uneducated person,' said Donald, ' like myself could feel at ease in his company . . . I am not a young man, but I would willingly walk ten miles every week for the privilege of hearing him.' Donald deeply relished Mr. Spurgeon's sermon on ' Absent Thomas ' and found in it many wholesome lessons.

The man who stood higher in his estimation than any other, however, was Dr. Hugh Martin, Edinburgh. This divine, who wrote and spoke so profoundly on such subjects as the righteousness and sufferings of Christ, appealed to him not only on account of his theological weight, but also by reason of the searching analysis to which he subjected the ground of each man's hope before God.

Donald Duff had his Bethel seasons, and one of these was at the Creich communion in the summer of 1872. On that occasion the Lord's people present were so sensible of the gracious Spirit of God in the ordinance, that one old man from the parish of Reay prayed publicly on the Monday morning for grace to endure the pain of separation. ' The Lord was there.' The services on that Sabbath began at eleven in the morning and, with an interval of one hour, continued till half past nine at night. After the services the people refused to disperse, and continued in praise and prayer till midnight. The following day they gathered again at seven in the morning. The Highlands has had but few days like these since, when the Lord shined gloriously out of Zion.

Perhaps the next most memorable communion ever held in the north was at Dornoch about the year 1831. The following quotation describes the heavenly power which literally melted down many of those who were present.

'The fourth table which held sixty communicants, was wholly filled by young converts from Tarbet, Ross-shire, who had been brought to the knowledge of God in a spiritual revival a year or two before. When the service was over the linen cloth was as wet with their tears as though it had been taken out of the sea. Soon afterwards a deadly plague of cholera broke out at Portmahomack and made almost a clean sweep of this crop of young converts. Angus Murray, Dornoch, said of them that the Lord took them away with Him to Heaven " soft and warm as they were!" ' But we are speaking of Donald Duff.

As may be seen from the following extract from one of his letters his own quiet meditative exercises also brought him much blessing. ' I was meditating lately on that passage where the Bride of Christ compares her Beloved to an apple tree among the trees of the wood, and speaks of herself as sitting under his shadow. She found a shadow in His incarnation and humiliation, a shadow in His obedience and sufferings, and a shadow in His intercession. And His fruit was sweet to my taste. She tasted the sweetness of a word of pardon dropped into her guilty conscience, the sweetness of a word of love dropped into her trembling spirit.'

How Donald himself stood in the estimation of his contemporaries may be inferred from the following incident that has come down to us. In 1878 he was at the Dornoch communion. Dr. Kennedy opened the Question on the Friday. It was based on the words, ' But I see another law in my members warring against the law of my mind' (Rom. vii. 23). The doctor offered an opening exposition in his usual profound and comprehensive manner; but afterwards he and others would give the palm to Donald Duff for an unusual insight into the nature and motion of original sin as it stands in the light of God's law, and as it affects the new man whom God had saved by ' the law of the Spirit of life in Christ Jesus.'

The word ' consecration ' had not been introduced into the Christian vocabulary of his day; but this is how he defined a Christian. The Bible, he said, speaks of four classes of men. There are the men of Belial. For them to live is sin. There are the ' men of the world,' and for them to live is the world. The third class are those who may be outwardly religious, but self interest or self esteem is the spring of all they do. For such to live is self. The man who has passed out of these states, leaving even the garments which clothed him behind, is the man in Christ. To this man Christ is so precious that he counts all else as dross for the excellency of His knowledge. ' For such to live is Christ.'

Having in his own words lived ' in four counties ' he became acquainted with the most eminent of the ' Men.' The man who attracted him most was David Steven of Bower, Caithness. He looked upon David as the ' last rose of summer,' or as a green branch which the sea had carried high up on the beach, and which could give one an idea of how high the tide of true godliness had once risen in Caithness.

The writer once met a Christian lady in Stratherrick who remembered Donald. One day she observed him looking over a wall watching a cat that brought all its feline cunning into play so as to catch an unwary bird which flitted among the ferns. Donald was fascinated and remarked, ' That is how the evil one catches souls.'

A minister in the north was anxious to hear a sermon from the words: ' My God shall supply all your needs.' On a Monday of a communion in a certain parish he read the chapter which contained those words at family worship. Donald was present and prayed. In his prayer Donald touched on the needs of the poor in spirit, and the unsearchable riches which are in Christ for such. Later in the day this minister intimated that Mr. Duff would preach in the evening. To his joy he took the words as his subject. As he spread his wings to this great theme it was evident that he was on the eve of entering in to possess his inheritance above. That, in fact, is the last glimpse we get of him in his public ministry.

Donald Duff passed away early in 1885. A friend who ministered to him in his last hours told him that many of his friends had written to enquire for him. As their names were mentioned he tearfully remarked, ' I feel their prayers around me.' When asked if he had a message for them he said, ' Tell them that I find it is well that I have not now to begin to seek the Lord; for the time of trouble is assuredly not the acceptable time.' He spoke very tenderly of the sufferings of the saints, and how many of them entered the river rejoicing in the hope of the glory of God. For many hours he lay in a state of unconsciousness; but a few moments before he entered heaven he opened his eyes. They shone with the bright lustre of an unearthly light as if he saw beyond the earthly scene the fringe of that eternal world of glory for which he had longed. It was left to his friend, Mrs. Auld, of Olrig, to give poetic expression to the great blank which the death of this prince with God had caused. Here are two of her verses:—

> Our shepherd, our father,
>   Hast gone to his rest.
> Oh, Death, will naught serve thee
>   But that which is best?
> Thou hast ravaged our Highlands;
>   Thy scythe has cut down
> Our princes, our nobles,
>   And men of renown.

> Then sure there is reason,
>   We sit sad and lone;
> Amid the world's music
>   Ariseth our moan.
> Those stars, where was mirrored
>   Jehovah's own light,
> Have departed for ever—
>   And left us in night.

There were two other Donalds in Badenoch whose reputation for gifts and graces was almost equal to that of Donald Duff. The one was Donald Cattanach; the other was Donald Ross. Donald Cattanach lived in the world of thought and prayer. The spirituality of his conversation revealed his heavenly mindedness. A minister who knew him personally once said that he had never seen a man who could walk with a surer step among those altitudes of Revelation which treat of Divine sovereignty, predestination, and the Person and work of our Lord. In his own eyes, however, he was as one who knew nothing and deserved nothing. For that reason he walked the whole way to the city that hath foundation with his head bowed, a debtor to the grace which flows from the merits of Another.

He was only eighteen years when John Kennedy, Killearnan, first called on him to speak in public. Half a century afterwards his son, Dr. Kennedy, called on him to speak on a similar occasion in Dingwall. The large congregation present observed that when Dr. Kennedy stood while Donald was speaking he was only paying an exceptional tribute to a man eminent above many as a witness of Christ.

We close this chapter with a short description of a ' Men's ' meeting held at Auchterneed—the scene of Donald Duff's labours in the past—in the summer of 1880, a few years before he died. Such meetings were occasionally held in the district between services during summer communion seasons. The account given of this particular service is from the private Diary of Margaret Nicol, Resolis.

Conducting the meeting on this occasion was the worthy Mr. Gilmour, resident lay agent at Strathpeffer. The singing was conducted in the traditional way. But Ross-shire's sweet singer and Doctor Kennedy's favourite precentor—Angus Macdonald, Urray—was no longer present. After several of the men had engaged in prayer, Mr. Gilmour exhorted the company in the words of Peter: ' But grow in grace, and in the knowledge of our Lord and Saviour, Jesus Christ.' The good man goes on to say: ' Will any grow but those who have grace? Yes; men may grow in knowledge, they may grow in ability to speak, they may grow in boldness and presumption, and have no grace. But all such growth is of nature only. But what is grace? Grace in God is an unfathomable ocean of favour and mercy. In the creature it is a principle of life planted in the heart in regeneration. It is kept alive and nourished by God breathing upon it. Grace enables its possessor to do those duties towards God which otherwise he could not fulfil. Grace in the soul discovers our inward depravity and helplessness. It destroys our self-sufficiency. Thus the roots of a true child of God grow downward in humility and dependence on the sovereign grace of God. As grace grows in the soul the old man is crucified. There is also a growth upwards. If his roots, like those of Lebanon, go down, he shall also " grow up as the lily."

' Those who are young in grace are often happy. They rejoice in what they hear when God's Word is preached. They rejoice in what they read in God's Word. They rejoice in what they feel in their own heart. Therefore they are apt to say, " O! if I live for twenty or thirty years in God's service what joy and happiness I shall have! " But they little know what is to follow. God will not suffer them to have their roots in these frames and comforts. They soon discover that sin is in all their members, and they abhor themselves before an Holy God. The world draws them down to itself and they cry, " My soul cleaves to the dust, quicken me according to Thy Word." Sin now becomes their daily bondage and they cry out for deliverance. This cry is the evidence of God's life in the soul, and of an inward growth in grace. When they find their hearts and minds going out after the poor trifles and vanities of time to the neglect of the great concerns of the soul and Eternity they cry out for more holiness and truth in the inward parts. Where are their roots *then*? Only in the everlasting Covenant of Grace which is ordered in all things and sure. In our outward walk, however, the world should see in us an uprightness which it cannot gainsay. The natural conscience of Saul made him weep over the uprightness and love of David whose life he himself would have destroyed . . .'

In this way the excellent men of our Highlands brought forth out of their treasures things new and old.

The Two Great Separatists.

JOHN GRANT, Strathy, and Alexander Gair were, by common consent, the two great Separatists of the far north. Their lives are well known. It would be difficult now to pick up any fresh information along a path so frequently trodden in the past.

Walter MacKay, who used to teach and preach in Waternish, Skye, over eighty years ago, once told his friends of how when, in the pangs of unbearable conviction, he consulted the famous Alexander Gair. Alexander listened to Walter's story. When he finished he began to tell Walter of his own rough passage into the place of refuge. As Gair ended the terrible narrative of his spiritual sufferings the other felt that, by comparison, his trial was light indeed. Walter expressed his fear that beside the trials which Alexander had to endure he had no conviction worth mentioning. The reply was characteristic: ' My lad,' said Gair, ' if God made you bleed, ask not that you should be felled with His hatchet.' (' A ghille, ma leig Dia fuil asad, na iarr thusa fuille na lamhach.')

Sandy Gair's comment on the secret of victory in the Christian life is equally characteristic. ' When Saul was at war with his enemies he made a vow that he would not eat till he had gained the victory, but Jonathan ate of the honey and gained the victory. If we were eating of the honey of the promise we would enjoy greater victories over our spiritual enemies, but we have more of the spirit of Saul than of Jonathan.' His way of illustrating man's spiritual restoration was also memorable. ' A man,' he said, ' had a bad watch which would work now but stop the next time. He sent it to Inverness, but it came back as bad as ever. He tried Aberdeen and Edinburgh but with no better speed. One day he opened it and discovered the maker's name and address on it. At once he sent it there and got it back in perfect order. Do this with your heart when none else will heal it. Come with it to its Maker.' This saying shows a deep insight into the Christian secret of relieving and removing the tensions, mental conflicts, and spiritual disorders which are common to many of God's people. 'He restoreth my soul.'

In this Sandy Gair was not a mere theorist. His own painful trials he brought to God and found healing in the Tree of Life. He could therefore comfort the afflicted soul. Once he met a Christian woman who was writhing in the grasp of a powerful temptation. Aware of her state and its cause he said: 'Poor woman, you are lying there in your misery. I was looking for your case for thirty years, and did not find it till now.' His kind and reassuring words, bathed in Christian sympathy, brought relief. Having travelled the same dark road, he knew how to guide her to the door of hope.

In a letter to a friend he lifts for a moment the curtain which hid his inward brokenness. 'It is long,' he wrote, 'since my lot was cast in the 88th Psalm . . . and this new dispensation has brought me forward to the last three verses. My wound is deep, but His wounds are sweet. I am sure my stroke is heavy; but it might be heavier if He were to mark iniquity . . . You will find me also in the 109th Psalm: For I am poor and needy, and my heart is wounded within me. I am gone like the shadow when it declineth . . .'

Although Sandy Gair was a Separatist there were those whose pulpit ministrations he valued. He listened once to a soul-nourishing sermon. Afterwards he spoke of nature's process in producing milk, the most nourishing of foods. The cattle feed in the meadow and drink from the stream, and, by a wonderful process, this nourishment becomes the best of foods.

And that sermon, derived from the life-giving pastures and streams of God's Word, and coming through the spiritual process of prayer and meditation, was 'the sincere milk' to nourish his spirit.

A man from Ness, Lewis, who frequently visited Caithness following his calling as a fisherman, used to tell a story of a blossoming young divine who once preached in Wick in the great tent erected for the Gaelic service. At the end of the sermon the young man, in egotistical vein, gave a favourable verdict on the quality of his own effort. The mighty Separatist, who sat near the pulpit, was up like a shot. 'I am,' he said, 'climbing toward fourscore years, and they have passed like a tale that is told. I hope also to be in everlasting glory with the Lord where a thousand years in His Presence will be as one day. Yet I hope that I shall not feel the past time or the future eternity put together as long as I felt this wearisome service.' If the word was hard, we hope it had the effect of pruning the pride of a novice.

Equally apt and memorable was 'a grace after meat' uttered by Gair. His companions were in a hurry, and they asked him to be brief. In his native tongue he said, 'Their Thu ruinne gu bheil sinn crionn,' agus bu dual dhuinn; ach is Tusa Mac Athair nam fial, agus bu dual dhuit. Tabbhair dhuinne dhiot fein na ni 'ar ceangal ruit, oir gus an toir Thu ni dhuinn, cha toir sinn ni dhuit.' ('Thou sayest of us that we are meagre in what we give Thee, and from such a stock we came; but Thou art the Son of the liberal Father, and Thou art as He is. Give us of Thyself what shall bind us to Thee; for until we get from Thee, we can give Thee nothing.') Slightly different versions of this remarkable invocation have been given; but the rhythm and originality of the above—as it used to be quoted in Sutherland—were very characteristic of Gair.

Some have misrepresented the 'Men' as abstracted, and often idle, mystics whose interest in the supernatural world make them neglect their temporal affairs. But it was not so. The evangelical faith does not drive men into grim monastic cells to escape the tasks and trials of life. Rather it made men respect God's appointed work for man on the earth, however humble. The 'Men' were, therefore, as a general rule, practical Christians whose quickened conscience would not suffer them to come under the reproof of God's Word as in the case of those who do not work. The story of Sandy Gair in his tussle with a man of the world over the price of a cow may throw some light on this point! The baffled would-be buyer of Sandy's cow said: 'You men are strange. You say you are not of this world, and yet it is more difficult to do business with you than with other men.' Sandy's illuminating reply was: 'Though you are fools enough to leave Heaven entirely to us, we are not such fools as to leave the whole of this world to you.'

If there were those like Sandy Gair who left the Church, there were others, less militant but equally pious, who remained within its pale because they believed a called and converted Christian ministry was a divine institution. The relationship between the evangelical ministry in the north and many of the most eminent among the men was tender and lasting. To illustrate this unbroken loyalty to the Church let me tell one story of an old man in Sutherland. Stricken in years and living a long way from the Church this choice saint appeared one stormy day at the service. His minister, amazed to see him, asked him why he had ventured abroad in such weather. He said: 'I had the mind to come, and God gave me the strength. I also thought I might be of some help to you here. Besides I did not want to grieve the Spirit of the Lord by seeing my place empty in His house.' What a contrast to the lapsed luke-warm spirit of our age.

Of John Grant I shall relate but one story which came down to us through the late Professor J. R. MacKay. It may serve to show that under John's stern and rugged exterior there throbbed a heart which was at once tender and affectionate. In the village of Dunbeath there was a good man of the name of John Sutherland, who once invited John Grant to his home so that his friends might have the benefit of his conversation on Scripture and Christian experience. In due course John arrived at Dunbeath, but being quite unaware of the reason why so many had gathered where he lodged he remained silent. Afterwards when he heard how sorrowful the company were over his remissness he was much grieved. He tearfully chided himself for his apparent coldness among so many of the Lord's people. ' If,' said John, ' I had spoken then of the love of Christ, who knows but we might have been so bound together in that love that I would even come to love the birds which flew from Dunbeath to Strathy. But I was brutish in having sealed my lips.'

Christian affection was a reality in those days. At a meeting in a Caithness village the conversation turned on the subject of how charity would seek to cover a multitude of sins. The love of Christ in the soul would always seek to hide the infirmities which it might see in some of the Lord's people. An aged Christian woman present was asked to give her view on this point. She said: ' My love for the people of God is such that, if I could, I would hide their infirmities from the Lord Himself.' ' O woman,' said one present, ' this world is no place for you.' Before many days had passed she was taken to the place where love is perfected.

This spiritual tenderness in relation to one another and to the cause of God was nourished and cultivated at the Throne of Grace. The evangelical ministry of that generation could preach with freedom and power, being strengthened by the prayers of many hearers. In the burgh of Dornoch the minister once was so manifestly enlarged through the prayers of the people that a person present exclaimed: ' O the wonder! one man preaching and the rest praying.'

There was, by the way, another man in Sutherland of the name of John Grant. He lived at Grimachdarry in Kildonan; and he must have come across his Strathy namesake, who also lived there in the days of Mr. A. Sage. Mr. A. G. MacLeod, Free Church minister at Croy (1859-92), tells a story of how, as a mere lad, he accompanied the Grimachdarry John on a fishing expedition. As the son of the local schoolmaster young MacLeod could fish the river. A pretty but poor girl in the district was getting married, and John was anxious that she should have something worthwhile for her marriage reception. Coming to a pool in the river John said: ' Now, my boy, you go on and I will go behind this rock and offer a word of prayer.' After several minutes the boy appeared with a large salmon which leaped clean out of the water to the grassy bank. ' Now, my boy,' continued John, ' you go again and I'll retire to pray.' In two minutes the lad hooked a salmon which took him an hour to land. ' Now, my boy, we shall go home. By the good providence of God we shall not return empty-handed, and the bride of Badenloch will not want a salmon for her wedding feast.' This incident shows that the ' Men ' were not stern, rigid legalists who frowned on the lawful enjoyments of life. They were holy in their conversation here, but they were also, as a rule, kind and intensely human. John loved ' the boy,' and after listening to his first sermon he remarked: ' Now, my boy, I am not displeased with you; but you must come down to things about the hands. It is there the devil does the harm.'

When John Grant, Grimachdarry, passed away, his white pony used to surprise its new owner by stopping dead at those places where its first master used to dismount for secret prayer.

'The Great James' and his Friend.

IF some of the 'Men,' like those whom we have just named, have been honourably mentioned in our evangelical literature there were also some excellent men of whom little notice was taken.* Let me mention just two of these. The first is James Matheson, Clashnagrave, Dornoch, and the other his close friend, Angus Murray, Balloan, Dornoch. James was a man apart. When awakened by God's spirit his sense of guilt and his apprehension of God's wrath were so deep and prolonged that for many weary months he refused to sleep lest 'in hell he should lift up his eyes.' Although he afterwards enjoyed a measure of sunshine in the way, the terror of that early time never wholly left him. He ever stood in awe of the infinite holiness of the Triune God. His sin was ever before him, and he could never think of it without exclaiming with the prophet: 'Woe is me! for I am undone; because I am a man of unclean lips . . . for mine eyes have seen the King, the Lord of hosts.' He never enjoyed the strength or assurance to profess the Lord in the ordinance of the supper. If he had a lowly estimate of himself, he was high in the esteem of his brethren. He once dined with Dr. Kennedy in the Dornoch manse. When James afterward stood up to pray the doctor went down on his knees at his feet. Listening to him that afternoon one present remarked: 'It would be a wonder if the like of James Matheson would arise in seven

* This chapter was written a number of years before Dr. Munro's excellent book, "Records of Grace in Sutherlandshire," was edited. The several anecdotes mentioned in this chapter are so identical in substance that the author decided to make no change.

generations.' His mental conflicts were often severe. During one of these he was tempted to put an end to his misery. But He who gave a commandment to save His people arrested his footsteps with a word from heaven. He could never again pass that place without falling down on his knees to praise his Deliverer.

James Matheson lived almost literally on his knees. Hard by the burn which ran near his home there was a hollow. Long after he had left the earthly scene the marks of his knees could be seen where he had so often wrestled with the Angel. His abstraction in prayer was so great that at one time he failed to hear the cries of his friends who were looking for him in a wood. He was so long away that they got anxious about his bodily comfort. When at last they found him in a secret place of prayer it was as if he had been sojourning in another world. If at times he surprised his friends with ecstatic exclamations about 'the glorious beings' whom he sometimes saw where the Gospel was preached they knew that he had reached a place in the Christian life far beyond themselves.

His habit of praying outside till very late at night sometimes wearied his housekeeper, who, as a rule, read the Scriptures at family worship. One such night she decided to retire to rest. When at last James came in he called to her. This he repeated three times, without receiving an answer. On the following day he rebuked her, saying: ' Last night as you were sitting by the fire Satan came into your company and suggested that as you were tired you should go to sleep without worship. I came in and asked you three times if you were asleep, and you made no reply, though you heard me well. Now, let me tell you that God is to show you mercy; but before you taste of His mercy you will have a year of bondage in your soul for every time I asked you that question.' Shortly afterwards this girl was convicted of sin and three years elapsed before the Lord loosed her bonds.

Someone once tried to encourage James to profess his Lord in the Sacrament. ' Look at that man. He was a great sinner, and yet he professed.' ' That person,' James would reply, ' is a true jewel of God.' ' But look at that woman,' encouraged his friend. ' Was she not a great sinner also? ' ' Yes, but she is now one of Christ's doves.' ' Is it not a proof then that you have the Spirit of God yourself when you know so well who are His children? ' James answered, ' The devils knew them and their Lord on earth, but they shall never share in His mercy.' This reply is an indication of the torments of fear which this much tried man had to endure in this life.

An instance of his mystic nearness to the unseen world may be given here. One day he came in from his place of prayer in a very distressed manner. He startled the company by informing them that six men had just been drowned outside Helmsdale, and of the six three had entered a lost eternity. The other three had gone to God. This was one incident in James's life which so greatly puzzled Archibald Crawford, whose Christian experience was more normal.

In his severer trials, and especially when writhing in the toils of unbelief, he valued the sympathy of his friends. There was one such friend who kept the door open for him night and day. If James happened to arrive in the night he would be asked the question, ' Who is there? ' The password was: ' Tha an cealgaire mór ' (' Who but the great hypocrite ').

The unchangeableness of God in the covenant of grace was his strong consolation in his manifold trials. A brief but memorable prayer which he once offered in public greatly impressed one who heard it: ' Glory be to Thee for what Thou hast been; and for what Thou art, and for what Thou art going to be to all eternity.' It was on this sure foundation that he placed all his hope.

If his conception of sin was just and scriptural no less was his conception of Him Who came to make an end of sin.

Thus he once said that the infinite greatness of Christ was seen in his ability to drink the cup of infinite wrath of the infinite God. In other words only the eternal and infinite God in our nature could drink that cup of wrath due to us for sin.

There was no man in the community whose word was more respected than his. The word might be severe, or it might be kind. In one home he took the father of a large family aside, and in a loving tone he asked him to show great kindness to one of his boys—a healthy lad of eighteen summers. He told the parent that for this young man life's candle was almost spent. Not long afterwards this youth was, as James believed, taken away to be with Christ.

There was another young man who sneered at his remonstrance against his desecration of the Lord's Day. 'Beware,' said James, 'lest the Sabbath should break you.' The young man concerned perished in tragic circumstances on a Sabbath morning.

I shall give but one other instance of the universal respect in which this good man was held. When the Dornoch Cathedral was being repaired the bones of some that had lain within its precincts were dug up to be reinterred elsewhere. The grieved and indignant James warned those engaged in the sacriligious work against disturbing the graves of the dead. The work came to an immediate standstill.

On the west coast of Ross-shire a young woman by name, I think, Ann MacKenzie, once decided to cross the moor to the Dornoch communion. Ann was in distress of soul at the time. On the way she asked the Lord to show her a sign for good. And this was how she conversed with herself in the way: 'If,' she mused, 'James Matheson will give out to read the 13th chapter of John at the meeting, I shall take it as a sign that there is still hope for me.' In the morning she attended the meeting, but to her dismay another man, the good David Ross, was in the chair. He gave out a chapter from the Old Testament.

At that point James stood up and asked David Ross to read the 13th of John instead, 'for,' he said, 'unless I am mistaken there is a poor soul present who is to get comfort from that chapter.' Ann MacKenzie could never forget how the Lord had, without human means, revealed her case to this good man.

This sympathy and communion which obtain in the Body of Christ may be illustrated by an incident in the life of another Highland girl. This was Jessie Russell, who lived at Dores, in Inverness-shire. Jessie was blind, and therefore could not read. There was, however a lady in Inverness who had a strong urge to send Jessie her copy of Elizabeth West's *Memoirs*. Though her mind reflected on the absurdity of sending a book to a blind person a voice continued to repeat, 'Send it! Send it!' The boy who appeared later at Jessie's humble abode told her that the post had given him a small parcel addressed to her. When the book was unwrapped Jessie asked the lad to give her some idea of the kind of book it was. He opened at random and read a page. The paragraph which he read referred to a severe temptation through which Elizabeth West had once passed. It so happened also that Jessie Russell was passing through an identical trial, and the words read proved to her to be 'a breast of consolation.' This by the way.

The joyousness and more balanced outlook of his friend, Angus Murray, often acted as a corrective to James in his trials. During one of his last visits to James's house he found him torn by 'manifold temptations.' His very face mirrored the depth of his mental anguish. A true son of consolation, Angus spoke kindly to him about the death of the Redeemer, and how by His dying on the tree He purchased eternal salvation for His people. Gradually but perceptibly the look of fear on the sufferer's face left him, and hope and peace again looked out through his eyes.

The words inscribed on James's stone of memorial—'These are they who came out of great tribulation'—truly express the earthly pilgrimage of a man who reached the prepared rest through fire and stormy seas.

We mentioned Angus Murray. Let us look for a moment at the rural and spiritual setting in which we first find this lively and attractive Christian. It is summer. The countryside is in its prime. A visitor approaching Dornoch that day could hear the soft ebb and flow of a Psalm which, judging by the volume of sound, is sung by a great multitude. The people worship in the open air. Angus Murray, then a lad of twelve years, sits in that vast congregation. John Kennedy, Killearnan, is the preacher, and his theme is the loveliness of Christ. 'Thou art fairer than the children of men' (Ps. xlv.). As the preacher goes on to describe the altogether lovely One the boy is quietly affected by the beauty which his inner eye sees in the Glorious Person so wonderfully portrayed in the sermon.

The sunlit sky and the green fields, as he afterwards told one of his friends, 'darkened' in comparison with the excelling glory which he saw in Christ, the Sun of Righteousness. He felt his soul being drawn away in unutterable love towards the Lord Jesus. The experience was not that of a young imagination overwrought by a vision which was soon to fade. So real was his conversion that for seventy-eight years afterwards Angus Murray lived a Christian life of singular depth of knowledge and undeviating devotion to the Lord and His cause. His attachment to God's people was his next outstanding characteristic.

In those days the land rejoiced in the presence of many who were noted for their eminence as Christians. Some of those had lived in the days of 'open vision' in the north. They were, in the words of the Prophet, the olive berries on the top of the uppermost boughs after the gleanings of harvest. Angus Murray made a round of the country that he might get to know some of those. He called on John MacIntosh, Farr. The veteran catechist received the young disciple in a manner which was in keeping with the way the older 'Men' sometimes tested the younger.

'The parish of Farr,' he remarked, 'was once worth coming to, for in it were those who were the salt of the earth. There are few of these now. This, indeed, is a fine day for hypocrites; they can walk abroad, and there is none to detect them. But it is a sad day for God's poor people.'

Such a stern reception was enough to discourage any youth, and Angus could only bow his head. Later on in the evening, after worship had been conducted, the old man melted, and became a bundle of affection. Before they separated John said, 'The words with which I greeted you, you must not apply to yourself. Let me tell you that as soon as I heard your footfall outside the door that truth came powerfully to my mind: " Fear thou not; for I am with thee: be not dismayed for I am thy God: I will strengthen thee; yea, I will help thee; yea, I will uphold thee with the right hand of My righteousness." And now that we are united in the Word of God eternity will not separate us.'

The measure of Angus's affection for the aged saint may be understood from the fact that on an evening he would stand outside his own home at Balloan and look up at the evening stars which he imagined were above John MacIntosh's house. As he said to a friend, 'I loved the stars which I thought were shining above his home.' In this way did these men fulfil 'the new commandment.'

Before John MacIntosh died Angus visited him again. As he kneeled in prayer at the bedside of the aged man, the words, 'The God who answereth by fire let Him be God,' powerfully affected his mind. In his prayer he mentioned the sin of Adam, and how God answered him by the fire of his just wrath. Then he was given an overpowering view of Christ as the substitute bearing the sins of His chosen people, and God answering Him by the fire of the wrath which they deserved. The glory, the love and the sufferings of Jesus moved his heart so as to make utterance almost impossible. When the prayer was ended the old man embraced his young friend. 'It would be well for me,' he said, 'if I got in five years what you received since you bowed your knee in prayer; but I was once as you are now. What you now enjoy, and more also, is reserved for me when I pass over.'

On his journey Angus was asked to call on an aged Christian woman, Elizabeth Sutherland. As he began to pray with her he felt as if a 'wave of power' had passed over his spirit. He prayed in much comfort. During his prayer Elizabeth would sigh audibly, and in bidding her farewell he expressed his concern that he was speaking words without knowledge, and therefore deserving of her pity. 'No,' she answered, 'but I pity you since you are going to live in a generation who shall not understand you; nor will you understand them.' Christian experience and discernment, in other words, were on the wane.

The quiet manner in which Angus Murray was brought into the Kingdom so early in life did not, of course, agree with the experience of all believing Christians. Some there are who must wait long at the base of the mountain which cannot be touched, and the summit of which is wrapped in darkness. Others escape the storm, and come to Mount Zion without hearing the dread 'voice of words.' Angus once heard one who laid down a rigid rule that a despairing passage through the Slough of Despond must necessarily precede a true work of grace in the heart. The remark threw Angus into a state of great anxiety. Was his hope before God the hope that maketh not ashamed? He went aside, and asked God to give him the needed knowledge of his wrath against his sin. His prayer was answered. As he afterwards told a friend, a flash of that wrath passed through his being. 'And if it had lasted for a minute instead of a second I felt my very reason would have given way.' He then understood that God had not appointed him to wrath, but to obtain salvation by our Lord Jesus Christ.

The late Professor J. R. MacKay, a man of great theological depth, once said that he heard Angus Murray in public prayer touching heights relative to the doctrine of the Atonement which threw more light on that awesome mystery than anything which he had read either in patristic or Puritan theology. When Angus in his prayers warmed to the congenial theme of Christ's love and sufferings ('an gradh agus na fulangais') his hands would unconsciously wave, and his tears would freely flow.

It was characteristic of men like Angus Murray that while they would continue long in secret prayer their public prayers were, as a rule, brief. In public they tried not to weary either God or man with much speaking. In Sutherland as many as twelve men would engage in public prayer and still keep within the canonical hour and thirty minutes. An instance of brevity in public prayer may here be given. A friend of Angus, James Munro, stood up to pray once in Dornoch. All he said was: 'Glory to Thee that Thou art God and not man, and that we are men and not devils.' A woman present whispered in the ear of a friend her disappointment at such a brief prayer. 'Do not say so,' said the presiding elder who overheard the remark, 'for you have heard a prayer which made Heaven rejoice, but which caused a frown in hell.' Another worthy, the excellent David Ross, would sometimes pray thus with the others, 'O nach d'thig Thu' ('O do Thou come').

A young lad once listened to Angus saying grace. The vivid and lovely words he carried in his memory to the end: 'Thou didst lead Thy people out as far as Bethany, and lifted Thy two hands above them and blessed them. And these two hands are stretched out above their heritage to the end of time.'

With such praying men in the pew the minister in the pulpit could not but feel strengthened and helped.

Mr. George Mackay, minister at Fearn, used to tell his friends of a service he once conducted in the Great Glen. During the opening prayer he suddenly found himself emerging out of extreme spiritual bondage. When he opened his eyes he saw that during the prayer the excellent Hugh Mackenzie, Glen-moriston, had arrived at the service. Hugh, as usual, arrived with his soul bathed in prayer, full of the love of Christ, and ready, like Hur of old, to uphold the wearying hands of God's messengers.

But, needless to say, God's blessing was not confined to the public means of grace. Several men in the vicinity of Dornoch were once returning from a meeting of prayer. On the way home they decided to call on a bedridden old woman known locally as 'Widow Mackay.' One of the company sympathised with her in her loneliness. 'But I am not alone,' she quietly answered. 'There were Four of us here this evening, and I was the only sinner among them.' By the other Three she meant the sensible presence of the Triune God. The man was so affected by her words that he turned aside to weep over his own comparative remoteness from God.

A much tried Christian minister once told a friend how Angus by a Scriptural remark on one occasion provided him with the key to Christian resignation and patience. Pouring his complaint into Angus's sympathetic ear, the latter quietly repeated the words of Psalm 34: 'But the Lord delivereth him out of them all.'

When the hour came for Angus Murray to leave this world his friend, David Ross, came to see him. His sufferings were so severe that David prayed for his immediate release. 'Leave him not long as he is, but take him Home speedily.' Thus David prayed. The answer came at once, and this good man departed to be for ever with the Lord.

'The Secret of the Lord.'

IN previous chapters we have touched here and there on an aspect of Christian experience which many regarded as 'The secret of the Lord.' The words are from Psalm 25. 'The secret of the Lord' was, indeed, a phrase often found on the lips of the more exercised believers of those days. Dr. Kennedy has a remarkable sermon on the words. In his sermon he deals in an interesting way with the several means by which the God of heaven may enlighten His people with respect to particular issues in Providence or Grace. The means by which He does this are manifold; but never does the method or matter of illumination offer any violence to God's inerrant Word, or to the experience of God's people in former ages. The communication of the divine mind to the soul is the office of the Holy Spirit, and the written Word is the chief means by which He reveals His 'secrets' to His own people.

Those who walk with the Lord by faith, and who know Him as their Companion in the way, cannot fail to enjoy intimations of His love and care. To such He is not silent. To such He is not a stranger. For their comfort and guidance He seals His promises on their heart in the power and efficacy of His grace. In His sovereignty He may elucidate and interpret for them some of His ways in Providence. Thus in Christian experience of any depth there is often an element of mystery and wonder unknown to the world, or to those who have only a name to live. But all these impressions and intimations, however genuine and precious in themselves, are subordinate to the Bible as a final and full revelation of God's mind. The apostle Peter speaks, for example, of those seasons 'on the mount' where they heard the voice from Heaven, and where they saw the Glory of the Lord. It was to them a day of heaven on earth. But he goes on to remind the Church that there is 'a more sure word of prophecy; whereunto ye do well that ye take heed as unto a light that shineth in a dark place, until the day dawn and the day star arise in your hearts' (I Peter 1). In other words, the written Word in its entirety is the great foundation of faith. God's secret with His people is but the evidence of their faith, and a token of their reconciliation and acceptance in the Beloved.

In this brief chapter we may mention one or two aspects of this secret; but since the subject is both delicate and mysterious one would need to approach it with a great measure of restraint.

There was in the north a young man in whose father's house the Lord's people were sometimes wont to meet. When, in their conversation, they touched on God's dealings with them, he found their language very strange, as if they were relating the happenings of another world of which he knew nothing. They would tell one another how, at times, they would awake out of sleep with God's Word in their mouth. They never doubted that when it came in this way it came from Above. It was a word which came in answer to prayer and which they needed to sustain them in some trial. It might come as a word of encouragement or warning. It might, on the other hand, have to do with some impersonal dispensation in Providence or grace. They believed the tidings were from God because, in Bunyan's phrase, they came with the sweet and wholesome taste of heaven upon them. Not only so but often they saw their fulfilment at the appointed time.

Let me give one or two examples of this. Charlotte MacKay, of Strathy, was a woman of unusual nearness to the Lord. At the end of her life she confided to a younger friend that she seldom awoke without the Lord meeting her with His Word on the threshold of the day. In this way God shined on her path to the end. This guidance from heaven and this daily supply of hidden manna, imparted freshness and fragrance to her life. With the Psalmist she could say, 'When I awake I am still with Thee.' But she was only one of many with whom the Lord conversed in the way.

There were others like Annie MacKenzie, Tolsta, and Norman MacDonald ('Tormod Sona'), of Galson, who took everything to the Lord in prayer, and who seldom made their requests known at the Throne of Grace without the Lord sealing His answer, through the Word, on their minds.

One peculiarity of Highland religion was its association with the Dream World. The Bible makes it clear that God has access to our minds at all times, and that in every age He has instructed many of His people in this mysterious way. In the words of Job, He can seal instruction on the spirits of men both in their sleep and in their wakeful hours. Thomas Goodwin makes the remark that God is the only Teacher who can impart knowledge to His scholars in their sleep. This mystical intercourse between God and His people, we believe, continues. It was, for example, one mode of operation by the Spirit in apostolic times. There is no instance in Scripture of any of the saints who doubted the validity and meaning of significant visions and dreams which they knew had a bearing on their own life, or on the life of others. Paul gives us an account of 'visions and revelations of the Lord,' when he wants to show the reality of his communion with the heavenly world. God, as in the case of Solomon, gives many gifts and blessings to His loved ones in sleep (Ps. cxxvii.).

It was an excellent Highland minister, the Rev. D. MacFarlane, of Dingwall, who once wrote these words in his diary, 'Dreamt a little before I woke this morning that I was in the company of some of the Lord's people, and that I was asked to return thanks after meal . . . Feeling myself a great sinner my mind opened to the wonderful way of salvation by

grace very soon after I began to speak, and I felt really happy. It
was only a few words that I said, and concluded with the words:
" Whoever heard of such a gracious way of salvation? There
never was anything like it in the past and there shall never be
anything like it in the future. It stands alone among God's
works." I awoke with great comfort and praised the Lord for
showing me anew the way of salvation in my sleep . . . I was
taught to know the Gospel awake, and the Lord revealed Himself
several times to me in my sleep. This was a sweet savour to my
soul, so that I could say, " I love the Lord."

There was in Sutherland a good man, Mr. MacKay, Saval,
who often prayed for the enlargement and revival of God's
Zion, and who, in a day of small things, was greatly encouraged
by a dream which he believed came from God. It was in the
year 1926 that Mr. MacKay dreamt that he saw a tree studded,
in gold lettering, and on which were inscribed seven historical
and prophetic dates. The dates indicated periods of time between
1560 and 2016. The seven periods coincided with the condition
of the tree at the time. In 1560 the tree was healthy and
flourishing, but in 1660 it had begun to decay, till in 1940 it
had almost entirely withered. But by 1960 the tree was beginning to revive rapidly till in 2016 it had flourished into a noble
tree, fresh, strong, and lovely beyond any tree he had ever seen.

By means of this symbolic vision the godly Mr. MacKay
believed that the Lord had given him a wonderful view of the
Church in God in the world from the Reformation to the coming
of that promised day when Zion, revived and raised up by the
outpouring of God's Spirit, shall again became ' a noble vine,'
the glorious branches of which shall overspread this world in
which Christ died.

Mr. C. H. Spurgeon was in his day greatly loved in the
Highlands. His incomparable sermons could be found in every
place where the Lord had His witnesses. His death sent a pang
of sorrow to the hearts of many who loved him as the greatest

exponent and defender of Evangelical Calvinism. With his passing away a bright star had vanished from their sky. On a Sabbath night in January, 1892, a man was praying up in the island of Harris. When late that night he rejoined his friends they saw that he was weeping. In answer to their questions as to the cause of his grief he said, ' Spurgeon is gone.' The following day a message reached the island that Spurgeon had ' gone Home ' at the very hour in which this good man on his knees in prayer, had seen his spirit wrapped in light and accompanied by a great host ascending up to heaven.

Of a different character is a remarkable, though not rare, experience related by the late Rev. Angus MacKay of Kingussie. The story appeared in the monthly magazine of the Free Church of Scotland in February, 1926. It is that of an invalid, but eminently godly woman—Peggie MacLennan—from Aultbea in Ross-shire. Peggie, who was of a very reticent disposition, had only told about her ' vision ' to three people in thirty-five years; for like another ' she kept these things and pondered them in her heart.' ' When,' wrote Mr. MacKay, ' we reached the house we found Peggie sitting by the fireside with a peculiarly solemn expression on her face, which gave me the impression that the Glorious God was her fear, and that His light gave her brokenness of heart and contrition of Spirit that are pleasing to Him. Through patiently persevering in questioning I got the following information about her vision.

' When she was about twenty years of age on a communion Sabbath in Aultbea, in June, a bright sunny day, between two and three in the afternoon, as she was alone in the house, a man, dressed all in white came in through the open door and saluted her, saying: " I see you are alone." " Yes," she replied, " but I am not alone now."

' Then he took the Gaelic Bible which was lying on the table and assumed a sitting position, but used no chair. He read the twenty-third Psalm, and sang it all in melodious strains, Miss

MacLennan joining in the singing as she had never been able to do before. He then read the first chapter of Second Peter, after which he prostrated himself with his face very near the floor, and prayed very earnestly. Then rising, he exhorted her to be faithful and promised that he would come again, and that her heart would rejoice.

'After pronouncing the benediction he bade her goodbye, shaking hands with her, and she felt his hand like the hand of a man. She followed him as he went out and observed with wonder that he went up from the earth in front of her door. I asked her how she felt over this experience, and she said: "I feel very unworthy."

'Peggie MacLennan's name will ever remain fragrant in the memory of all the Lord's people who knew her.'

But such things as these may not belong to normal Christian experience, and we are not seeking to prove anything in mentioning what is, perhaps, the more mystical side of the spiritual life. All believers have their own 'secrets' which they prize as their Lord's tokens for good to their souls, and which, like a heavenly treasure, they hide in their heart.

In conclusion it may be asked why the spiritual life in our Highlands has so much declined in the last eighty years. Some may ascribe this to the dispersal of the people, the lingering death of the language with which the good days of Gospel power were associated, or to the adverse impact of a new age on a people susceptible to new impressions. Others would say that through an unconverted ministry the advent and blight of the liberal theology has, like the boar out of the forest, wasted God's vine in the Highlands as in other places. Allowing that much may be said for all these opinions, it may also be that, like others before us, we ourselves have sinned the blessing away.

About fifty years ago the crew of a boat from the island of Skye put in one Sabbath day at Loch Eriboll, on the north coast of Sutherland. They had hoped to hear a sermon. But there was no service held. An old Christian woman on whom they called said: ' We now get a service once in four or six weeks. Many of the witnesses are gone. This is the parish where Mr. John Kennedy laboured. This was a favoured spot once; but the Lord in judgment has taken His witnesses and His blessing away because when we had them we failed to value them.' It is the old sad story retold: 'He turneth a fruitful land into barrenness, for the wickedness of them that dwell therein ' (Ps. cvii).

But here we shall draw the curtain over the window through which we have for a moment looked on the past with its lovely story of God's grace. We have only mentioned a few of the great company of believers who lived and died in the faith which is in Jesus. And who would not pray with one of them: ' O! to be of them, and to be with them? '

> ' Chum fios bhi aig an al ri teachd,
>   A chlann a ta gun bhreth;
> 'S gun innseadh iad do'n linn nan deigh
>   Na nithe sin fa leth ' (Ps. lxxviii. 6).

EVANGELICAL RELIGION IN THE SCOTTISH HIGHLANDS

Douglas MacMillan MA BD

**Professor of Church History
Free Church College
Edinburgh**

EVANGELICAL RELIGION IN THE SCOTTISH HIGHLANDS

I   From the Roman Legions to the Reformation.

The beginnings of vital Christianity in the Scottish Highlands go back such a long way that they are hidden in the mists of antiquity. All the indications are that although the trained legions of Rome could not subdue the warlike tribes of ancient Caledonia with the sword the gospel of God's grace brought them, early in our era, into obedience to the Prince of peace.

When and by whom the Evangel was first brought into our northern glens is not clearly known. However, it is not unlikely that among the Roman soldiers left to defend the great wall which extended from the river Forth to the river Clyde, there were earnest Christians who, as opportunities arose to talk to the people of those northern tribes, would tell them the message of "Jesus Christ and Him crucified".

The Celtic Church

The first certainties that the early history provide for us focus upon a fine Christian missionary called Ninian. Born around the middle of the fourth century, he was actually a native of the region and, before the Roman Legions had taken their final departure, he had visited Rome, spent some time in Gaul with the famous Martin of Tours, and set up a Christian centre on the shores of the Solway. From its famous White House - the Candida Casa - Whithorn takes its name still.

While the Whithorn church was being built, news came of the death of Martin, and the new building was dedicated to him. As the death of Martin occurred in A.D. 397 it helps date the time of Ninian's mission and the erection of the first known Christian church in Scotland. The monastery at Candida Casa was known as the "Great Monastery" and it became a college for the training of missionaries. Students flocked to it from all quarters and men who trained there went out and missioned in Ireland and into the North of Scotland and have left traces of their work in local place names as far north as Glenurquhart on the shores of Loch Ness, and Navidale in Sutherland.

Columba

Though many earnest missionaries worked northwards from Whithorn in the fifth century, the name which stands out most prominently in the emergence of the Celtic Church is that of Columba who landed on the island of Iona on 12th May 563. The teaching of this zealous missionary who, with his disciples, had crossed over the Irish sea, was warmly evangelical and under his labours the North and the West of Scotland became the cradle of a robust, literate Church which in its best days sent many Christian scholars and preachers out across Europe.

This is not the place to dwell on the forces which eventually obscured, and almost extinguished, the witness of that old Celtic Church. It is enough to say that under the invasion of Norse paganism, and medieval Roman Catholicism, the darkness of a long spiritual night settled over the Scottish Highlands. The Word of God became a closed book to the people, and many of their instructors in spiritual things were not only ignorant of Scripture in the letter, but were without any experience of its sanctifying power.

Precisely how the gospel made its way back into this Northern region of Scotland after the Reformation is also a perennially interesting question but one whose answer is not easily determined. While much that is instructive and thrilling has been recorded about the reintroduction of the gospel and the noble figures involved in the process to the south of the Grampians, all too little is recorded in this connection by those

who lived to the north of that great mountain range. The
Psalmist of Israel could say:-

"O God, we with our ears have heard,
Our fathers have us told,
What works Thou in their days hadst done,
Ev'n in the days of old." (Ps. 44.1)

Today, we can only deeply regret the silence of our Highland
forefathers of the immediate post-Reformation period on this
important subject. It would seem that those who had the ability
to write up the history largely lacked the opportunity and,
however desirable they themselves may have regarded such a
work, they were intent rather on the practical tasks which lay
to hand and demanded their energy. So our knowledge of the
Highland church has to be gleaned from sporadic writings and
a wide variety of scattered and, for the main part, secondary
sources.

Wycliffe's Bible.

The time came when the deep spiritual darkness that had
overlain Scotland through the medieval period was pushed aside
and a new day of gospel light began to dawn over the land.
But unlike the beginnings of the Celtic Church, when the light
had come out of Ireland in the West, it was from the Continent
in the East that the brightening rays of a new day took their
rise. With the establishment of the Reformed Church in Scotland
in the summer of 1560 the new day had come. That Church
faced an enormous task and not the least of its difficulties was
that it had still to reach Westwards and Northwards into the
remote and mountainous regions of the Highlands before the
Reformation of religion in Scotland was complete.

Over the previous thirty years, however, it would seem that
Wycliffe's Bible and Tyndale's translation of the New Testament,
as well as the powerful Protestant tracts and theological writings

of Martin Luther, were penetrating the land along the commercial routes from Germany and the Low Countries. The ports of the Eastern seaboard such as Leith, St. Andrews, Montrose and Aberdeen gave the Reforming literature access to the Scottish Lowlands. In the same way, those of Inverness, Cromarty, Tain, Wick and Thurso gave it entrance to the North-east Highlands. When the great evangelical doctrines that informed, and gave impetus to, the Reformation process began to impress the English-speaking people of those regions, it was natural they would tell their Gaelic-speaking neighbours what they had learned and experienced of God's grace. In that way, gospel light began to penetrate the districts around the Northern seaports.

Patrick Hamilton

Tertullian, one of the great theologians and writers of the Early Church, gave us the dictum that, "the blood of the martyrs is the seed of the Church." The Scottish Reformation brought martyrdom to a number of Christians and among the earliest of them was Patrick Hamilton. An aristocrat by birth, he was given the income from churches in the North to help finance his studies and was Provost of the church of Tain and Abbot of Fearn from the age of twelve.

The young Hamilton went to Paris University about 1515 and graduated five years later, soon after Luther had taken his bold stance for the gospel. He returned to work in St. Andrews University but coming under suspicion of Lutheranism there early in 1527 he fled to Wittenberg and, for a period, actually worked alongside Luther. He was at the opening of Philip of Hesse's new Evangelical University of Marburg (May 30th, 1527) and drafted the theses for the first academic disputation. Later that year he returned to Scotland, intent on preaching the gospel, but was enticed to St. Andrews and burnt at the stake there on 29th February, 1528 while still only in the twenty-fifth year of his life.

While there is no evidence to show that Patrick Hamilton ever preached in the churches of Tain or Fearn, the people of that area, like those in the Lowlands, must have heard of his martyrdom and the memorable words uttered by him in the flames, "How long, O Lord, will darkness cover this realm, how long wilt thou suffer this tyranny of men? Lord Jesus, receive my spirit." His death certainly had a different effect from that anticipated by those who caused it, for one man is reported to have observed that the "reek (smoke) of Master Patrick Hamilton had infected as many as it blew upon." His death would raise many questions in the North-east and stir a special interest in the book, and the doctrines, for which their brilliant young Abbot was willing to give his life.

II   From Reformation to Covenant; 1560 - 1638.

The history books inform us that men of high position gave their influence to establishing Reformation principles in Scotland. This was true not only in the South but in the North as well. Thus, in the Scottish Parliament of August 1560, all the Commissioners from the Grampians right up to the North Sea voted for the disestablishment of the old, moribund Romish Church and the ratification of the new Reformed Confession of Faith prepared by John Knox and his fellow- Reformers.

Prominent among them was John Grant, chief of that clan, and Commissioner for the county of Inverness-shire. For the county of Ross, there was Robert Munro, 17th Baron of Foulis, and also chief of his clan. William Innes of Innes, Sutherland of Dufus, the Abbot of Fearn; the Commissioner for the Burgh of Banff, and the Commissioner for the Burgh of Inverness; the Earl of Caithness; and John, 15th Earl of Sutherland. We also know from Knox's History of the Reformation that Lord Lorne, or

Argyll, was very active in support of the Reformation. Such men were linked, by ties of blood, with leading families right through the Highlands, and the clan chiefs in those days wielded a mighty influence for good or evil among their people.

Another person whose influence must have affected the area north of the Highland line was the Regent Moray, half-brother to Mary Queen of Scots. He was thoroughly committed to the Reformation cause, and with vast landed interests in Moray and Ross, must have exercised a strong influence in those areas. The enthusiasm of the people of Easter Ross for Protestant principles at this early period finds unusual testimony from him, for he presented an oak pulpit to the parish church of Tain sometime before his assassination in 1571.

Donald Munro of Kiltearn

At the Reformation there was a great dearth of Reformed ministers in the Highlands but the new Church showed real enterprise and, as early as 1563, special Commissioners were appointed to plant churches and schools. By 1567 there were 257 ministers in Scotland, 455 readers, and 151 exhorters - 863 in all.

The Northern Highlands shared the benefits of those special measures and one of the Commissioners selected in 1563 was the Rev. Donald Munro, the minister of Kiltearn. He is said to have been the first minister to have preached the Reformed doctrines in the North at a service which, traditionally, is said to have taken place "in the old Church of Limlair, between Dingwall and Foulis" (Dr. Donald Munro; *Free Church Monthly Record* July 1918, p.116). This famous minister is described by the historian of the period, George Buchanan, as a "learned and godly man" (The quotation comes from the Moderatorial Address of Dr Gustavus Aird in the *Proceedings of the Assembly of the Free Church*, 1888, p.5). We have only a meagre knowledge nowadays of the men who occupied the Highland pulpits prior to the beginning of the 17th century but one historical record again involves the burgh of Tain, and interestingly, confirms the beneficial influences that trace back to the Regent Moray and Patrick Hamilton. Of the nineteen ministers that were present at the famous Aberdeen Assembly which met, under the frown of King James VI, on 2nd July 1605, one was the Rev. John Munro, the minister of Tain. He must have been thoroughly Reformed and thoroughly Presbyterian into the bargain to have risked incurring the Royal displeasure in such bold fashion.

Robert Bruce in Inverness

In the year 1605 another event took place which was to strengthen and advance the spread of the gospel in the North in an unusual and unexpected manner. The minister of St. Giles, Edinburgh was the famous Robert Bruce of Kinnaird, a masterly theologian, a powerful preacher and probably the most popular minister in the Scotland of his day. His preaching was greatly owned of the Lord and one of his converts was none other than the great Alexander Henderson, architect of the National Covenant of 1638 and a Scottish Commissioner to the Westminster Assembly of Divines in the following decade.

Bruce is undoubtedly one of the greatest men of his time, and even King James himself professed the highest esteem for him. In 1590, when James went to Denmark for his Queen, it was Bruce who was left in ultimate control of national affairs and James acknowledged his obligations to him. Perhaps Bruce had demonstrated his leadership qualities only too well, however, for a few years later when he opposed the introduction of prelacy into the Scottish Church by the King, he was banished North of the Grampians and "warded" in the town of Inverness. Bruce entered Inverness on the 27th August 1605

and was to spend almost eight years there. He had freedom to
preach every Sunday forenoon and every Wednesday evening.
There is little doubt that he attracted many people to those
meetings and that his preaching was blessed to some. Released
in the Spring of 1613, he was forced into a second exile in
Inverness on 18th April 1622. It was while he was setting out
on this last journey to the Highlands that he had one of those
remarkable moments of prophetic, spiritual insight which
various writers speak of in connection with his ministry (Cf.
Chapter 19 "Seeing Visions and Dreaming Dreams" _ in D.C.
MacNicol's fine biography, *Master Robert Bruce*).

The following account of this particular incident has been
well attested by one of his successors in Larbert and recorded by
the historian, Wodrow. "When Bruce was going to Inverness on
one of these occasions, several gentlemen and relatives
accompanied him part of the way. Ere he entered the saddle he
stood looking up to heaven musing for a few minutes: after he
had mounted, a friend asked him how he was engaged when
musing? Mr. Bruce replied, 'I was receiving my commission from
my Master to go to Inverness, and He gave it to me Himself
before I set my foot in the stirrup, and thither I go to sow a
seed in Inverness that shall not be rooted out for ages.'" (*Life
of Bruce*, Wodrow, p.146).

On this second visit the effects of Bruce's preaching were
remarkable. Dr Aird is clearly surprised, but deeply impressed,
by the impact made on this occasion far to the North and West
of Inverness. He writes, "It is upwards of half a century since I
heard a tradition which astonished me then, that during part of
Mr Bruce's ministry in Inverness, persons from Sutherland and
Ross were in the habit of going there to hear him, through
bridgeless streams and rivers, and across ferries; but years
thereafter I found it verified in "*Blairs Autobiography*." He then
goes on to quote Blair as follows, "June 29, 1700.- The memory
of that man of God, Mr Bruce, is sweet to this day in this place

Inverness. He in the day of James was confined in this town and country about, for multitudes of all ranks would have crossed several ferries every Lord's day to hear him, yea they came from Ross and Sutherland: the memory of the just is blessed." (*Proceedings of the General Assembly of the Free Church*, May 1888, p.6).

Speaking also of this second period of Bruce's Inverness ministry, Donald Munro says, "A great revival of religion took place under his earnest, evangelical preaching. A few of his converts in the faith, it is said, were alive at the Revolution (1698). Sometimes it happened that men that came to Inverness on business were drawn by irresistible force to Mr Bruce's meetings. On one occasion a drover from a Highland glen was led to attend the week-day service, where a barbed arrow entered his heart, which forced him to cry out in his broken English - 'I'se gie two coos [all he had] to 'gree God and me.' But the Lord also gave his devoted servant souls for his hire among the nobility. It is said that the Covenanting Earl of Sutherland was one of the fruits of his ministry, as also his Countess, a daughter of Lord Fraser of Lovat - one who was eminent for her deep piety." (*Monthly Record* July 1918, p.116).

Alexander Munro of Durness

One of those converted through the ministry of Bruce at Inverness was Alexander Munro, son of the Laird of Katewell, Kiltearn. This fine young man was ordained into the ministry in the extensive parish of Durness in the north-west of the county of Sutherland. He found his people illiterate and ignorant of the Gospel but he persevered in teaching them and Dr Aird says, "Wodrow in his *Analecta* states that, At his entry there the people were almost heathen, but his labours had great success, and a large harvest of souls." (op cit p.7).

One interesting feature of this ministry has come down to

us and it well illustrates how ready those early Highland ministers were to turn every facet of life to spiritual advantage. Noting how fond the people were of singing Gaelic songs their young minister capitalised on their aptitude for poetry and began to versify portions of the Scripture into their native Gaelic, setting them to popular tunes and teaching them to the people through the winter evenings. In such interesting fashion were his parishioners made familiar with the fundamental doctrines of God's Word, and many of them came to experience its power.

Highland soldiers in the Netherlands

Yet another influence upon the emergence of evangelical life in the Highlands can be traced to the wars of religion on the Continent. As early as 1586, 1603, and 1628 Scottish soldiers were being enrolled into what eventually became known as The Scots Brigade. The Stuart policies of imposing Episcopacy made it easy for such military contingents to get good Scottish ministers to serve as chaplains. The practice can be illustrated from the fact that Rev. Andrew Hunter, minister of Carnbee, Fifeshire, was one of the early chaplains listed on the payroll of the Scottish regiment serving in the Netherlands.(Cf A.L. Drummond, *The Kirk and the Continent*, p.78 ff.).

The armies involved on the Protestant side were often favoured with some of the finest of the English Puritans - great biblical scholars and warmly evangelical men - as their chaplains. One fine study of this fascinating connection informs us, for example, that, "In spite of some unworthy chaplains, the religious situation in the seventeenth-century Netherlands army was better because of the well-motivated refugee Puritans available for service, some of considerable theological eminence (William Ames, Robert Parker, John Burgess, John Paget, Thomas Scott)" (Keith L. Sprunger, *Dutch Puritanism* p.263).

It was actually from the northernmost point of the Highlands that Sir Donald MacKay of Naver, afterwards known as the first Lord Reay, mustered the initial expedition of Highland soldiers for this purpose. In 1626, along with Munro of Foulis, he gathered over 2000 men, composed of MacKays from his own lands in the West, Sutherlands from the Eastern parts of the territory, and Rosses and Munros from the county of Ross and town of Inverness, and embarked at Cromarty for the Continent. After fighting with the forces of the King of Denmark, this regiment entered the service of the "Lion of the North", as the godly Swedish King was known, and in his service they so distinguished themselves that throughout the Netherlands they were spoken of as "the right hand of Gustavus Adolphus."

It seems to have been under the influence of the Puritan chaplains that a great many of those Highland soldiers were converted to Christ and large groups of them returned to their native counties as ardent Christians. In this way, the evangelical life of the Northern Highlands came under the influence of English Puritan theology, with its emphasis on personal, experimental and spiritual religion, as well as its strongly reflective and doctrinal character. The link is further illustrated in the common occurrence of the Christian name Gustavus through the northern counties; Dr Gustavus Aird, the Free Church minister of the parish of Creich through the latter half of the nineteenth century is said to have had several elders named Gustavus on his Kirk session through that period.

Dr Donald Munro, noting this Puritan influence and its impact in the North, goes on to say, "When one of those pious soldiers, as was sometimes the case, lived at a considerable distance from the parish church, he considered it his duty to conduct a Sabbath evening meeting, which the people in the neighbourhood attended. These gatherings are said to have been instrumental in the conversion of sinners and in the refreshing of God's heritage." (*Monthly Record* August 1918, p.132).

III   From the Covenant to the Revolution 1638 to 1688.

It is not surprising to find that the strong Evangelical testimony implanted in the North through the labours of Robert Bruce, and the influence of the godly amongst the returned veterans of the Continental wars, eventuated in the National Covenant of 1638 being largely and heartily signed in those northern counties. Though there may have been strong political motives for the excitement that this event precipitated through the country, yet its basic movement was undoubtedly that of a strong spiritual current; it was more the work of religion than of politics. And the Lord did not leave His people without gracious tokens of His evident approval, for the signing of the Covenant in the Highlands, as elsewhere, was followed by great spiritual prosperity.

We know very little about the ministry in the North in the years immediately following the famous Covenanting Assembly held at Glasgow in 1638, yet there appears to have been spiritual stirrings in many areas in the North, and these were fostered by the influences we have already noted, and in special meetings and conferences which multiplied through the next few decades. In the short memoir of Thomas Hog of Kiltearn, one of the famous ministers who was "ousted" at the Restoration, we have almost the only record of that period in the North. Great success evidently attended his own short ministry before his ejection, and probably the same happy results flowed from the ministries of other faithful men also.

There is an interesting reference to prayer and fellowship meetings amongst the Christian people of the North at this moment in their history which has come down to us in the correspondence of one of Cromwell's soldiers. It is part of a letter dated 8th January 1651, in which the writer, while mentioning some of the troop movements through various Highland areas, remarks, "I perceive by Captain Simpson and others that came from thence that there is a very precious people who seek the face of the Lord in Sutherland, and divers other parts around Inverness, which but that I have had it by so good hands, I should have much questioned, considering how few all the Southern parts have afforded... and though there were very few in any part of this nation wherever we came that would be present at any private meetings, yet the people in these parts will rather leave their own ministers and come to private houses, where our officers and soldiers meet together" (Donald Munro, *Monthly Record*, August 1918, p.132).

This illuminating comment is a fairly clear indicator, not merely of the spiritual hunger of those people and their desire for teaching and fellowship, but also of the scarcity of evangelical and bible teaching ministries in the North as compared with the South of Scotland where believers would not leave their ministers, and the regular, stated means of grace which they already enjoyed.

Of the 400 ministers who refused to conform to the demands for acceptance of Episcopacy in the wake of the Restoration of Charles II in 1660, few more than a tenth were to survive the Revolution which restored Presbytery and closed the Covenanting period. Of eighteen ejected in Argyll, only seven survived; of eleven in the North, eight, among them Thomas Hog of Kiltearn. By that time this godly man, and most of the other survivors as well, were not capable of carrying on their ministries, not so much from their age as from the permanent effects of rigorous persecution.

Notable Highland Conventicles

The work of Murdoch Campbell, which this sketch gives historical background, begins with eye-witness accounts of open-air Communion services in the Highlands. Such occasions were greatly used of God in encouraging Christian believers and in the conversion of sinners. It would seem that the sacrament of the Lord's Supper was seldom observed in the North by the "conforming" ministers who, to a very large extent, held the parish pulpits after the ejections of 1661. But there are two places which, traditionally, have been connected with great Sacramental gatherings in the North during the dark days of the Covenanting persecution.

One of these was at a place called Obsdale in the parish of Rosskeen in Easter Ross. There, on a fine September day in 1675, a huge number of earnest Christians gathered to observe the Lord's Supper. Three of the ousted ministers led the services, John MacKilligan of Fodderty (his wife had a small estate in Alness, where he preached through the years of his ejection; (cf. Kennedy's *The Days of the Fathers in Ross-Shire*, 1979 edition, footnote p.37), Hugh Anderson of Cromarty, and Alexander Fraser of Daviot. Dr Kennedy writes of this event, "Mr Anderson preached the preparation sermon on Saturday, Mr MacKilligan officiated on Sabbath in the forenoon, and Mr Fraser in the afternoon, and Mr MacKilligan preached the thanksgiving discourse on Monday. During this last service, there was such a plentiful effusion of the Spirit, that the oldest Christians then present declared they had never enjoyed such a time of refreshing before" (Op cit. pp. 38, 39. Cf also Wodrow's II, pp. 284, 285).

The other such occasion has an added interest for us today because of the unusual circumstances which led up to it. Although all the parish ministers in Sutherland had actually conformed and so, to a large extent, had lost the confidence of the people, a minister from Warwickshire found his way to the Cape Wrath district of Sutherlandshire. He was, in fact, the great- great grandfather of Dr Gustavus Aird, who has been mentioned already and on whose work this present narrative has drawn at various points.

The English minister, George Squair, himself a fugitive from Charles II's religious policies, became so concerned with the spiritual needs of the people that he set himself to learn Gaelic, and became an accomplished preacher in the language. His preaching through the Northern districts was greatly blessed and the time arrived when he proposed to hold a Communion.

The place selected for the purpose was, according to Dr Donald Munro, "an isolated spot among the wild hills of the parish of Eddrachillis" (*Monthly Record* op cit p.132). Another historian speaks of this Communion and tells us, "The whole service was a memorable one. ... Not only was there no interruption of the service, but all there felt so much of the Lord's presence, and their bonds were so loosened, and their fears so dispelled, that all, without a single exception, felt constrained to say with Thomas, My Lord and my God, and without exception, commemorated the dying love of their Redeemer" (Quoted by John MacInnes, in *The Evangelical Movement in the Highlands of Scotland*, p.155).

Such occasions will be mentioned again, for writers on the religious life of the Highlands recognise that, right through from these Covenanting days until the great Evangelical Awakening of the nineteenth century, the sacramental gatherings and the district "Fellowship", or "Question" meetings as they were called (and they were an invariable element of Evangelical Communion seasons) were amongst the main agencies in evangelism. "To one or other of them", says MacInnes, "we can trace all or most of the awakenings and revivals which have quickened the spiritual life of the people" (op cit p.155).

IV Out of Moderatism to Evangelical Awakening, 1730 to 1830.

The revivals of the 1740's in Cambuslang and other areas of Lowland Scotland worked northwards into the Perthshire

Highlands, and on beyond Inverness into the area of Easter Ross, Nigg, Fearn and Tain. While the North had its own share of Moderate ministers, who tended to be orthodox in theology but, as the name suggests, always very chary of religious enthusiasm or any emphasis upon spiritual life or personal godliness, there were also earnest gospel ministers of the best kind to be found in many parishes.

On the Western seaboard of the Highlands there were fewer instances of spiritual awakening through the first half of the eighteenth century than in the North, and by all accounts forthright evangelical ministries were few and far between in those parishes during that time. It was to be into the late 1700's and even the first decades of the 1800's before the gospel was to make its strongest impact in the West, and before many of its ministers could properly be reckoned amongst the great Highland Evangelicals. One exception is the saintly, (and physically huge) Aeneas Sage.

Ordained to the ministry in the parish of Lochcarron in 1726, this rugged man of God was destined to become one of the great folk-names in the history of Highland Evangelicalism, and was regarded by many with something of the awe of an Elijah. But his work, although ultimately greatly blessed, was never easy and must, at least initially, have been extremely difficult and exacting. On his very first night in his parish, his new flock tried, literally, to burn him out. He survived this attempt on his life and went on to change his people through his powerful, biblical preaching. "He found the people", writes his grandson, Donald Sage, "sunk in ignorance, with modes of worship allied to Paganism. Before the close of his long and efficient ministry, the moral aspects of the people were entirely changed." (*Memorabilia Domestica*, p.2).

Another powerful and influential ministry was also conducted in this same parish over the closing years of the eighteenth century and it had beneficial effects over an astonishingly wide area. Writing in 1861 Dr John Kennedy, Dingwall, in his well known book, *The Days of the Fathers in Ross-Shire*, says, "Of all the eminent ministers in the Highlands, none is more famous than Mr Lachlan Mackenzie of Lochcarron. Owing to his genius, his peculiar Christian experience, and his great acceptance as a preacher, he has retained a firmer hold of the memories of the people than any other besides" (Op cit pp.57,58). Lachlan Mackenzie was settled as the minister in Lochcarron in 1782 and his ministry was greatly blessed there, and all over the Highlands, until his death on 20th April 1819.

V   The Ministers in the Evangelical Awakening

The solid foundations which underlay the spiritual revivals of the mid-19th century, and the evangelical ministries that were able to guide and channel the masses of new converts into the paths of godliness, trace back into the early years of the century. As well as the great ministries of John Kennedy, Redcastle (father of Dr John Kennedy, Dingwall) and Dr John MacDonald, Ferintosh (known as The Apostle of the North because of his wide-ranging, itinerant, evangelistic labours) which attuned the ears and the hearts of thousands to powerful, doctrinal gospel preaching, there were also other factors at work.

Not least amongst these, were the strongly doctrinal, theologically informed, and intellectually stimulating ministries of Dr Andrew Thomson in Edinburgh and Dr John Love in Glasgow. These great city preachers were making evangelical teaching tell on the student world of their day, having their respective city charges crowded with divinity students, and the future preachers of Scotland's pulpits hung on their every word. Great preaching shapes men and influences future ministries, and of course amongst these students were many young Highlanders whose preaching, in turn, was to transform the lives of countless numbers in years to come.   The famous

brothers, Archie and Finlay Cook, for example, sat at the feet
of Dr Love through their student days in Glasgow.

Varied types of Gospel Ministries

The lengthened perspective from which we are able to look back
and survey the Highland religious scene through the first half of
last century helps in an assessment of the ministries that led to
the Awakening. It is quite clear that many of the pulpits,
especially in the district then covered by the Synod of Ross,
were filled by able, biblical preachers. They were men who, for
deep experience of a work of grace, for habitual nearness in
their walk with God, and for clear, full, and powerful
proclamation of Gospel truth have seldom had their superiors in
any Christian Church.

That those ministers had their favourite themes is quite
clear, yet they all took particular care to cover the entire
spectrum of biblical truth and to declare, very faithfully, the
whole counsel of God. Among them, as their sermons and
history show, were men such as Dr Angus MacIntosh of Tain
who gave great prominence to the breadth and spirituality of
God's holy law, and the dreadful peril of the impenitent sinner
as transgressor of its righteous demands. Yet it was said that
this man was never harsh in his preaching or statements of
such solemn truths. Kennedy of Dingwall, himself a masterly
preacher, made a wisely critical and discerning hearer of
sermons, and he remarked of MacIntosh, "If he sometimes used
a sharp razor, it was always well oiled" (Donald Munro, *Monthly
Record*, September 1918, p. 132).

The fact is that one of the most luminous features of
Highland preaching in that era was its *tenderness* and many of
the recorded sermons, or fragments of sermons, which have
been preserved and have come down through the oral traditions
of the people bear ample testimony to this fact. Those men were

true "pastors" of the flock of God and took individual, and personal, spiritual needs into their preaching.

Other preachers such as Dr MacDonald, Ferintosh, gave particular prominence to the glory of Christ's Person and the richness and freeness of the way of salvation. He was a masterly exponent of the doctrine of justification by faith in Christ alone. To this special emphasis, apparently so perennially present in his sermons as to be a characteristic of his popular preaching, Dr Chalmers, for one, attributed MacDonald's great evangelistic success. There were men also of the Rutherford stamp, who were masters at preaching gospel comfort and consolation to downcast Christian believers. Such a man, it is quite clear, was the Rev. Charles Calder, MacDonald's predecessor in Ferintosh, for it is said that he never wearied of "speaking from a full heart of the *love of Christ which passeth knowledge*" (Dr Donald Munro, *Monthly Record* September 1918, p. 162).

The highs and lows of Christian experience were given ample treatment by the outstanding preachers of the North as well. In fact experiential preaching was perhaps the department above all others where the great masters of the northern pulpits excelled. The marvellous minuteness which such specialists in spiritual analysis such as John Kennedy, Redcastle, and his son, John Kennedy of Dingwall, John MacRae (known as Big MacRae), Knockbain, and Archie Cook of Daviot, could describe and illustrate, not only the past history, but also the present feelings of exercised souls was, to their hearers, plain proof that they were true messengers of God. Some of them are dealt with, illustratively, by Murdoch Campbell in this book and it is evident that they were no more surprising, or foreign, to his experience than to theirs.

The preaching of some of these Highland fathers was almost invariably characterised by apt illustration and a natural gift for figure of speech. They painted vivid word pictures which came alive in the minds and hearts of their hearers and remained

with them for long after the preacher's voice had stilled. Those
familiar with the literature or traditions of Highland religious
life last century will readily think in this connection of names
like Porteous, Kilmuir; Lachlan Mackenzie, Lochcarron;
Finlayson, Helmsdale, and Francis Macbean of Fort Augustus
who was in many ways the Christmas Evans of the Highlands.
Listening to such preaching was a moving and memorable
experience and the stories, illustrations and even the framework
of their sermons lived on amongst the people for many years
after they had been preached.

VI   The Spreading Flame

One great disadvantage under which the Western Highlanders
laboured for a long time was the lack of the Scriptures in their
own native Gaelic. The first translation of the New Testament
into Scottish Gaelic did not appear until 1767, and the entire
Bible was not published in Gaelic until 1801. The only way in
which the people could have the Word of God read to them in
their own language until those dates was by immediate oral
translation. This the evangelicals amongst the Highland
ministers trained themselves to do, and it speaks well of their
linguistic abilities that almost all of them could readily translate
in this way. They had mastered the technique of reading directly
from English into Gaelic in a very accomplished and informative
fashion.

Such facility, of course, lends testimony to the truth that
those men were very familiar with the Word of God. It is also
a salutary reminder that most of them were well educated and
compare more than favourably with present day ministerial
accomplishments in the fields of language and literature. John
MacKay, the famous seventeenth century minister of Lairg was
deeply read in Dutch theology and so was able, during the
Covenanting period, to carry on a theological seminary for

young men going into the ministry. The MS sermons of John Balfour of Nigg reveal his constant use of the Greek New Testament and James Fraser of Alness, author of *The Scripture Doctrine of Sanctification* was a theologian and scholar of high repute (Cf MacInnes, op. cit, p.70.).

Two Helpful Societies

The Evangelical Awakening also owed a great debt to two Societies whose members, over many years, took a deep interest in the moral and spiritual welfare of the Highland people. One of these was formed into a corporate body as early as 1709 under the title, "The Society for Propagating Christian Knowledge". The other was instituted in 1725, and was popularly known as the "Royal Bounty". These Societies succeeded in establishing, even in the most remote corners of the North, schools and mission stations which were the means of teaching the people to read and write and of bringing the gospel to them. Many of the men who became well known ministers actually served their ministerial "apprenticeship" in such stations and the combination of teaching and preaching combined to form them into extremely skilful communicators.

To mention only one such mission station, that of Achreny in the heights of the parish of Halkirk, it is worth noting that its name is associated with some of the best known ministers in the evangelical life of the Highlands. Alexander Sage, Kildonan; Hugh MacKay, Moy; John Robertson, Kingussie; John MacDonald, Ferintosh; John Munro, Halkirk; and Finlay Cook, Reay all served in this station and, as young men, gained the practical pastoral experience from its varied missionary tasks that was to shape their later ministries along very useful lines.

Schoolmasters and Catechists

In addition to the preaching of the Word there was also the widespread practice of catechising. With the financial support of the Societies mentioned earlier, Catechists were appointed to many of the northern parishes and did excellent work in teaching the Bible and the fundamentals of Christian doctrine as set out in the Westminster Shorter Catechism. These men generally visited all the families in their district and would frequently gather the people into one home where meetings for prayer, discussion and preaching were held to round off the evening. It was usually the case, however, that the evangelical ministers never wished to have this part of their pastoral and teaching work done for them entirely by others, for it was a labour they regarded as particularly important, and which they often spoke of as being especially profitable and enjoyable for themselves. The godly James Calder, minister of Croy, records in his diary, under the date of 24th October 1762, "This day had a diet of examination. The house was crowded, the Lord was present, the duty delightful and edifying." (Quoted from Munro, *Monthly Record*, September 1918, p.163).

The Highland schoolmasters also made a great contribution to laying the groundwork of evangelical life in the North and West of Scotland. There were three types of school in the Highlands last century. The oldest and longest established was the parish school, often spoken of as the "legal" school, and in the main centres they did a very good work educationally and spiritually. Future ministers, such as John Balfour of Nigg, Dr MacIntosh MacKay, Dunoon, and Dr George MacKay, Inverness all served such schools in their student days.

Then there were the schools, in more remote areas, supported by the Society for the Propagation of Christian Knowledge. For years, the men serving those schools also worked as preachers or catechists in the mission stations, and so part of their support came also from the Royal Bounty, and the instruction of the older people as well as the children of the district was in their hands. From 1811, special Gaelic schools were instituted where instruction in the medium of their own language could be given to the young Highlanders. Many of those Highland schoolmasters, serving the different types of school, were men of outstanding godliness whose labours were wonderfully blessed both in the conversion of sinners and the upbuilding of believers.

So keen were many of the people to take advantage of the facilities provided by the Gaelic schools of 1811, and the opportunity afforded to learn to read the Word of God in their own language, that sometimes the grandmother and the grandchild sat on the same bench. In this connection Dr Donald Munro has recorded a fascinating story. "The teacher who conducted the Gaelic School in Glencalvie, in the parish of Kincardine, Ross-shire in 1815, had an experience that was probably unique. One of his scholars, a man of the name of Iverach, had seen three centuries. He was a young soldier of seventeen years at the time of the Jacobite rising of 1715, and such was his desire to have access to the treasures of God's Word that in his 117th year he joined the Gaelic class, and became an enthusiastic, and not unsuccessful pupil" (*Monthly Record*, September 1918, p. 163).

VII   Times of Refreshing

The half yearly (in some circumstances, annual) commemoration of the Lord's Supper became a major feature of Highland religious life and, especially in the nineteenth century, was a major factor in spreading spiritual blessing. These sacramental "seasons", as they were called, developed into a carefully structured series of services designed to help foster spiritual life and Christian fellowship in people who often had to live in isolated places, and maintain their Christian witness under difficult providential circumstances.

Such occasions, and the enormous crowds they attracted, provided a high point in the Christian calendar of these people, and served a similar purpose to the Christian Conventions and Conferences which have featured more and more in the Evangelical world of the late twentieth century. As Mr Campbell weaves much of his narrative, and his fine devotional writing, around such gatherings, this attempt at filling in the historical background to his work can be drawn to a close with some further details of what they involved and how, in the eyes of ministers and people, they were such a rich means of grace and blessing. They were frequently linked, also, to times of revival and spiritual awakening as at the famous Kirk o'Shotts revival in 1640, when the Holy Spirit was poured out during the thanksgiving service on the Monday, the final meeting of a Communion season.

The Fellowship Meeting.

In the Northern Highlands the Friday of each Communion season was devoted to "The Men's Meeting", so called because the elders and leading Christian men spoke at it rather than the ministers. This was also known as the "Fellowship Meeting" or following its Gaelic title, the "Question Meeting", so called because, a passage of Scripture was given out by one of the men, who each then spoke to the *question* of one's standing before God. This would be dealt with in a practical fashion and "marks" or "tokens" of those who were the subjects of a genuine work of saving grace were brought from personal experience and deliberated upon.

Such meetings were frequently the means of removing the perplexities of anxious enquirers and seekers after the Saviour. As they heard the inward workings and experiences of God's people being discussed, so their own spiritual questions and strivings were often dealt with and explained for them. The topics handled varied enormously from speaker to speaker and, as most of them were mature, exercised believers of long standing, the richly experimental quality of the individual contributions provided a means of comforting and assuring sorely tried or downcast Christians.

The origin of those meetings has never been clearly traced but is generally associated with the ministry of Thomas Hog, the Covenanting minister of Kiltearn mentioned earlier. He is known to have come under very deep distress of mind when a student at the University of Aberdeen. He was greatly helped in his difficulties when he and some other young men developed the practice of meeting together for theological discussion and Christian fellowship. It has been thought that this habit suggested the idea of the Fellowship meeting to him, and that he inaugurated them in the early days of his own ministry in Kiltearn. The similarity to the Disputation or "Quaestio" (The Latin term by which it is known), an oral and sometimes written exercises in scriptural exegesis for divinity students which might well have been familiar to men like Hog, is also too striking to ignore. However all that may be, those meetings certainly became a prominent and valuable feature in the spiritual life of the Highlands.

It would appear that the meetings, in their earlier format at least, were held in each evangelical congregation on the first Monday of each month at noon, and were rather in the nature of a family or private character than a public meeting; that is, they were purely for Christian believers aiming to help those who had professed their faith in Christ and were in the full communicant membership of the congregation. In some cases where there were real spiritual strivings or soul concern, seekers after peace in Christ were permitted to attend at the discretion of the eldership. The Fellowship meetings on the Communion Fridays probably also took this same form at their first appearance, but eventually they were open to all who wished to come and, indeed, became so popular they had to be held in the open air, as the church buildings could not accommodate the crowds after the years of the Awakening.

The Communion Seasons

There is little doubt that the Communion seasons were a means of deepening spiritual life in the Northern Highlands, and did much to foster a rare type of godliness. As in other times and countries through the history of the Christian Church the Spirit of God, poured out in revival blessing, brought people through very vivid spiritual experiences both in their conversion and in their walk with God. Many maintained a lifetime of intimate, daily, close communion with their Lord and knew what it was to have His will made wonderfully clear to them through the Scriptures. This aspect of spiritual life, so common then, so rare now, features strongly in Mr Campbell's writing and should encourage every Christian to such godly and private disciplines.

The sacrament week was the great event in a northern parish through the middle years of last century. It was anticipated with great interest not only by the elderly and the more serious in the neighbourhood, but even by the young and such people as, otherwise, took scarcely any active part in the spiritual life of the parish. All was preceded by days of special preparation. Not only were arrangements made for entertaining the visitors, but in the case of the Lord's people, there was a looking to God for the preparation of heart they wished for, as well as earnest prayer for the coming of the Spirit of God in power.

We shall allow Dr Donald Munro, whose early spiritual nurture was amongst Christian people who had lived through and personally participated in such times of awakening, and who had seen something of their sunset glory himself, to describe the scene of a Highland Communion Sabbath service to us in two of his wonderfully moving paragraphs. They provide descriptions which could only have been written by one who was a deeply appreciative eye-witness, and was himself a participant in the solemn enjoyment of all that was taking place.

"Seldom could one witness a more inspiring sight than the immense concourse that assembled on a sacramental Sabbath in the days of the fathers. Under the canopy of heaven they met, in some wooded dell, at the famous 'Burn' of Ferintosh, on the grassy sea-shore, or on the hillside in some natural amphitheatre which seemed to have been created for the purpose. The very surroundings often seemed to lend impressiveness to the solemn service, for sometimes there was no sound to break the stillness which brooded over the secluded spot save the sighing of the gentle breeze, or the boom of the waves as they rolled on to the pebbly strand. In front of the preaching-tent stretched two long rows of Communion tables, with their snow-white linen, around which a dense mass of people, sometimes amounting to several thousands, sat. The picturesque appearance of the vast gathering might appeal to the superficial observer, for some of the venerable-looking men were attired in blue cloaks, and others had wraps and plaids of various shades, while over the caps of elderly matrons were large muslin kerchiefs.

At the appointed hour, generally 11 o'clock, the presiding minister entered the 'tent'. He was generally one of the most outstanding preachers in the North, for as a rule only men of weight and experience, such as Dr Angus MacIntosh, Mr. Kennedy, Killearnan and Dr MacDonald, were asked to preach the Gaelic Action. This was what the sermon prior to the participation in Communion, was called and, generally, it dwelt on some aspect of the Atonement. The preacher came direct from the ivory palaces of secret communion, and the fragrance which accompanied him was diffused around. The very reading of the opening Psalm had a subduing effect on the assembled thousands, while the singing of it to one of their plaintive melodies, led by a choice precentor as the leader of the praise was called, was most thrilling. The prayer which followed, so fervent and unctuous, found a response in many a contrite heart. It must have been a most cheering sight which met the eye of the preacher as he stood up to announce his text. An earnest, expectant look was depicted on many a countenance, for not a few came there to hear a message from God. The prayerful atmosphere which pervaded the congregation was intense, and the preacher was conscious of it. From the very beginning of the sermon, in which the glory of Christ's Person and the merits of His atoning sacrifice were treated with rare clearness, fullness, and tenderness, the interest of the hearers was aroused; and as the subject was unfolded their rivetted attention showed how precise doctrinal distinctions and apt illustrations were appreciated. But as the service proceeded, the breathless silence, the awed look, the deep sigh, or the trickling tear indicated how profoundly the hearers were being impressed. Sometimes a wave of emotion would pass over the congregation, under which they would be bowed down as the ripe corn before the autumn breeze. At other times, as the preacher became more absorbed in his theme, and rose, as it were from peak to peak, in his upward flight, some in the congregation were carried away in ecstasy of soul - the things of time were receding, eternal things were so real that they felt as if transported to the very gates of heaven, and seemed to gaze through shining vistas into the celestial city" (*Monthly Record*, November 1918, pp 178,179).

There were times when the Communion services were very long as relays of believers came forward, sat at the long Communion table, and then rose to give way to another waiting group. Each "table", or "sitting", was spoken to in a "pre-communion address" and then, having partaken, they were encouraged to faith and godliness in a "post-communion" word of encouragement. Dr Munro says that, "an outstanding feature of the day's service was the concluding address, which followed the administration of the ordinance. That was a part of the day's duties in which many of the noted ministers of the North excelled. Most moving were the appeals to the unconverted, for they flowed from a glowing heart in a molten stream. Many of the Christians in Easter Ross in Disruption times (1843) could trace their first serious impressions to the concluding addresses of Dr Angus MacIntosh." (*Monthly Record*, Nov. 1918, p.179).

VIII Alexander MacLeod, Uig, and the Lewis Awakening of 1826

As Mr Campbell mentions the Rev. Alexander MacLeod of Uig several times, and because the early chapters of the *Gleanings* feature many who were the fruit of a continuing revival which began under this man's unique ministry, it may be helpful to give a brief outline of his life and usefulness in the Lord's work.

Alexander MacLeod was a native of Sutherland, being born in the Stoer area of Assynt and so entering into the rich spiritual heritage of these northern parts in which, as we have seen, the gospel had been powerfully at work for upwards of 160 years before his birth in the year 1786. His mother was a very godly woman and he was reared in a home where the fellowship of godly people was always warmly welcomed. His conversion to Christ took place while he was still only fifteen years of age, and he traced it back to a sermon preached by the Rev. Charles Calder of Ferintosh. It is on this he reflects as he writes, "Remember the feast you had in Dingwall, on a sacrament occasion, when you could not deny that you got Benjamin's portion of 300 pieces of silver and five changes of raiment" (*Memoirs and Sermons of the Rev. Alexander MacLeod*, p.5).

Earning his livelihood for some years in crofting and fishing, he eventually heard, and heeded, the call of God to the ministry and to that end took up study in Aberdeen in 1808. On completing his education he was licensed as a ministerial probationer in 1818 and ordained and inducted as minister of the Gaelic Chapel, Dundee in 1819. From there he moved in 1821 to the parish of Cromarty. He then received and accepted a presentation to the parish of Uig in Lewis and was inducted to the Charge on the 21st April 1824.

That date was to go down in the spiritual annals of Lewis, for Alexander MacLeod was to prosecute a powerful and wonderfully fruitful evangelistic ministry in the Island over the following fifteen years and, as a result, it was never to be quite the same again. A new day had dawned in its history. He left Lewis for Lochalsh and after seven years there, in 1846, was called to Rogart, a parish in his native county of Sutherland, where he died on 13th. November 1869 at the age of 83, after having completed fifty years in the ministry of the gospel.

On his arrival in Uig he was the first evangelical minister the people had known and he found them, although for the greater part in Church membership, sunk in gross spiritual darkness. On the first occasion of observing the Communion he noticed that practically every person in the parish, irrespective of belief or behaviour, sat freely at the Lord's Table, and became profoundly disturbed at such an unbiblical state of affairs. So deficient in spiritual knowledge and saving experience did he find his parishioners, despite their public profession of being followers of Christ, that he took quite drastic measures to try and jolt them into an awareness of their true condition. He deferred the observing of the Lord's Supper in the parish for two years and began to preach sermons on the necessity of regeneration and true godliness. His pulpit emphasis became very specifically and specially evangelistic, and it appears, he was especially gifted at this type of preaching. Gradually at first, and then more frequently, he began to see people becoming very deeply moved under the gospel message and in about two years time he found himself in the midst of a great spiritual movement.

When next the Lord's Supper was observed amongst his people, matters stood very differently. By then his preaching of righteousness, his emphasis on the need of the new birth, and his powerful expositions of the doctrine of Justification by Faith in Christ alone had, under the blessing of God's Holy Spirit, revolutionised the spiritual values and the religious perspectives of almost all in his parish. On this occasion, so great was the change that only six people came forward to sit at the Communion table though he judged that, by then, many more were truly converted and should have been there. Such were the beginnings of a spiritual Awakening in the Island of Lewis which has persisted, in ebbs and flows, until the present day.

Edinburgh 1989

Also published by
Christian Focus Publications

THE
DAYS OF THE FATHERS
IN ROSS-SHIRE

by

John Kennedy D.D.

This rare book, now reprinted, portrays by anecdote, narrative and analysis the vital piety of by-gone days in Scotland.